'59

The Story of the 1959
Syracuse University
National Championship Football Team

SYRACUSE UNIVERSITY FOOTBALL SQUAD, left to right; Front row—Trainer Pratt, Asst. Coaches Szombathy, Beyer, Shreve, Bell, Head Coach Schwartzwalder, Asst. Coaches Dailey, Pirro, Trainer Reichel, Team physician Dr. Barney, Equipment Manager Zak. 2nd row—Ericson, Sullivan, Weber, Rockiewicz, Applehof, Nichols, Anderson, Skonieczki. 3rd row—Youmans, Mautino, D. Baker, Yates, Bemiller, Tarbox, Lomey, Mambuca. 4th row—Gill, Sarette, Bowers, Caramanna, Hart, Sproule, Brazel, Heck. 5th row—Moran, Lemieux, Gilburg, A. Baker, Howard, Brace, Colella, E. Davis, Fallon. 6th row—Feidler, Laffey, Fitzgerald, Santoli, Sobul, Reimer, Thomas, Schwedes, Brokaw. 7th row—Francovitch, Spillett, Brown, Cholakis, Howell, Hilliard, Neary, Saylor, Bartlett. Top row—Manager Hoag, Stem, Bennett, Godfrey, Easterly, Sokol, Grabosky, Gerlick, Beckom.

Courtesy of Syracuse University Archives.

The Story of the 1959
Syracuse University
National Championship
Football Team

Gary Youmans *and* Maury Youmans

Campbell Road Press, Inc.

First Edition
03 04 05 06 07 08   6 5 4 3 2

The paper used in this publication meets the minimum requirements of
American National Standard for Information Sciences—Permanence of
Paper for Printer Library Materials, ANSI Z39.48–1984.∞™

Library of Congress Cataloging-in-Publication Data available upon request.

Produced and distributed by Syracuse University Press
Syracuse, New York 13244–5160

The authors can be reached at fiveninefootball@hotmail.com

Manufactured in the United States of America

To our father
Edward Morris Youmans
1909–2002
Who never missed a high school game we played in,
much to the chagrin of the referees,
and was always there when we needed him.

I remember that the most impressive thing about that 1959 Syracuse team was their defense. It was one of the best I've ever seen or coached against in all of my years. That team had a combination of power where they could stuff the run, and enough speed that they could go sideline to sideline. Syracuse ran down most of our plays to the outside. Also, when we tried to throw the ball they had tremendous pass rush and hurried our passer. If we did complete a pass, they had somebody around the ball all the time. It was an extremely well coached football team, the best I've ever seen, when it comes to total defense. Running, toughness, and the ability to rush the passer. They had no weaknesses at all."

—LEE CORSO
ESPN Football Commentator,
Maryland Assistant Coach, 1959

Gary Youmans was raised in Syracuse, played basketball at Ashland College (Ohio) and presently lives in the Syracuse area. He coached high school basketball in Florida, and coached professionally in the Continental Basketball Association (CBA) and in Canada. He is a sports marketing consultant and has owned a minor league basketball team. He is married and has one son, Matthew, who is a recent graduate of Ohio State.

Maury Youmans is a Syracuse University graduate and was a member of the 1959 Syracuse University Football Team. He was named to the 1960 College All-Star Team and went on to play defensive end for the Chicago Bears and Dallas Cowboys, retiring in 1965, after six years in the NFL. He was appointed to serve on the first Florida Sport's Foundation Board by Governor Bob Martinez and later became its Chairman. Youmans was for many years on the selection committee for the Hall of Fame Bowl, now known as the Blockbuster Bowl. In addition to a career as Director of Sports Marketing for Rosser, International, Inc., an architectural and engineering firm whose principals participated in the design of the Carrier Dome, he also consults for Geiger Engineering, the company who designed the roof structure of the Dome and Clough Harbour & Associates LLP, a civil engineering firm based in Albany. He and his wife, Betty, reside in St. Pete Beach, Florida, and summer on Wellesley Island, New York. They have 3 children and 5 grandchildren.

Contents

Preface

GARY YOUMANS

For me, writing this book was like tracing a great story from the past that I found interesting because of the people involved. It occurred to me while listening to the hours of transcripts that the richness and the fullness of our lives is often enhanced by the stories we each have to tell and by the enthusiasm exhibited in sharing those events with others. These stories that came from the people who were there in '59 are delightful. The honesty, the genuine love and respect, each person has for one another comes through loud and clear. While recalling their teammate Ernie Davis 44 years later, voices crack with emotion, remembering what a unique and wonderful person he was. The Syracuse '59 team was by in large, a group of average athletes that came together to become a great team.

Coach Ben Schwartzwalder and his trusted aides Roy Simmons, Ted Dailey, and Rocco Pirro are all gone now, but their lives dedicated to each other and sports, along with their hardnosed approach to foot-ball, makes for some interesting reading.

These young men at an uncertain time in their lives were pushed by a coach who challenged them to be the best they could be. They didn't let him down.

Acknowledgments

MAURY YOUMANS

Compiling this book has been a wonderful walk down memory lane for Gary and me. It could not have been done without the willingness of my former teammates and coaches to share their memories of the trip we took together to an undefeated season and a national championship. I wish I could have reached them all in the writing of this book.

A special thanks to Reggie Schwartzwalder, Thelma Dailey, and Ida Pirro. They are very special ladies.

We are totally indebted to the hours of typing by Kelly Youmans, as well as some editing by my old teammate from high school days, Tom LaRochelle.

A big thanks to Ed Galvin and Mary O'Brien and their folks over at the Syracuse University Library who were so helpful to us in researching this book, and to Pete Moore and Sue Edson at Syracuse University Sports Information a special thank you for going the extra mile in our search for pictures. Also, we would like to thank Maureen Reidel for her assistance in helping us move forward with this project. Finally, our deepest appreciation for the gang over at Syracuse University Press whose professionalism and help made this book a reality.

The authors of this book are personally responsible for all errors, misstatements, omissions, inaccuracies, commissions and embellishments, especially the embellishments. If it's wrong, it's our error.

This book could not have been written without the dedication and determination of my brother Gary. He spent long hours in the Syracuse University Library researching the information for this book. With that in hand he wrote the narration as I passed along the conversations I had with my teammates, coaches, and friends.

'59

The Story of the 1959
Syracuse University
National Championship Football Team

Practice begins. Courtesy of Syracuse University Archives.

1

Syracuse Begins Practice

On Tuesday, September 1, 1959, Coach Ben Schwartzwalder greeted sixty-eight players who would make up this year's Syracuse University football team. Schwartzwalder and his staff had a little more than three weeks to prepare this squad for it's first game of the season, September 26, at home against the Kansas Jayhawks. The team's first practices were greeted with temperatures in the mid-eighties, unseasonably warm weather for early September in central New York State. Although the team was loaded with returning lettermen from last year's 8–1 season, Schwartzwalder had one big problem: Who was going to play quarterback? Chuck Zimmerman, the starting quarterback for the past three years, and his backup, Dan Fogarty, had graduated. Senior Bob Thomas, the heir-apparent, was suffering from a bad back as practice began. After that there was not one player with any real game experience. Schwartzwalder was so concerned that he was considering moving last year's starting right halfback, Gerhard Schwedes, to quarterback. A third possibility would have been choosing between two sophomores, Dave Sarette and Dick Easterly. Unfortunately, neither had any varsity experience and thus were considered longshots. These next three weeks would be critical as the Orange faced a very tough schedule, and without strong quarterback play, the Orangemen could be in for a very difficult season.

In 1958, Schwartzwalder's team's only loss had been to Holy Cross, 14–13. Following the season, the ninth-ranked Orangemen were selected to play in the Orange Bowl against the powerful Oklahoma Sooners. Syracuse, now having gone to three major Bowl games in the past seven years, was starting to erase the stigma that Eastern college football was inferior to the rest of the country. A good performance against Oklahoma would begin building respect as a legitimate national power, something Syracuse coaches and fans had craved. Schwartzwalder's post-season Bowl record at Syracuse was poor. In the 1953 Orange Bowl, Alabama beat Syracuse, 61–6. Syracuse's next Bowl appearance, the 1957 Cotton Bowl, saw Syracuse lose a close game to Texas Christian University (TCU), 28–27. During that game, Syracuse's All America halfback, Jim Brown, scored twenty-one of his team's twenty-seven points. A blocked extra point proved to be the difference in the outcome of that game.

BILL BELL (Assistant Coach): "Jim Brown was an awfully young kid when we got him. I think he was just sixteen. He was a great athlete and a very intelligent person. He was probably the first free-thinking athlete we had up at Syracuse. We were practicing down below on the old practice field and every day he would come in and he'd be a half hour late. Finally I told him, 'Jim, I can't have this.' Well it happened again, and I went to Ben and I told him, 'Ben I can't coach this guy.' I said, 'He won't show up to practice . . . and you know we're going to have to do something.' Ben went to him and told him to go get his stuff and clean out his locker. He told him to go because we just didn't feel that he was an asset to our football team at that time but you know, he turned it around. He really matured his senior year, and damn he was an athlete! I hear them talk about these guys today but not a one of 'em could hold a candle to Jim Brown. He was the greatest. He had to be the best athlete that ever lived. You know the guy could have made a million dollars boxing."

As the Orange Bowl loomed, Schwartzwalder understood the importance of this game and decided to take his team to Raleigh, North Carolina for a week of hard workouts. The head coach wanted a place warm enough to be able to practice outside, but quiet enough that his team would be able to focus and prepare for a tough game. It had been almost a month since they last played, a hard fought 15–12 win on the road against West Virginia. Schwartzwalder knew his team needed the kind of physical practice only the outdoors could offer. He wanted his team to do some hitting. "To beat Oklahoma you need to be able to hit with them," he exclaimed.

Schwartzwalder wanted to put in a series of new plays for Oklahoma. Unfortunately, the openness of the North Carolina State facilities allowed for no real controls on who could observe their practices. He was unhappy with this situation and wanted his team practices to be closed. It was common during Syracuse's time in North Carolina for the head coach and his staff to scurry around checking on the people watching their practices to make sure no notes were being taken. It was not so much that Schwartzwalder did not trust Oklahoma. Bud Wilkerson, in Ben's opinion, was a class act. Two years previously Wilkerson had invited Syracuse to Norman to use Oklahoma's practice facilities in preparation for the Orangemen's 1957 Cotton Bowl appearance. Schwartzwalder trusted Wilkerson but he didn't trust those zany Sooner fans who, in his view, would do anything to help their team, including spying on the Syracuse team's practices. "They have fans all over the country," was his take from Tobacco Road. "Listen," explained Ben, "I wouldn't purposely spy on another team, but if someone wanted to give me some information about them, why sure, I would take it, and so would Oklahoma."

During their time in North Carolina, a boot camp atmosphere existed. Living in dorms and practicing twice daily didn't make a fun bowl experience for the team. Players were getting banged up, but Ben was determined to have his team ready for Oklahoma, and the coach stuck to his schedule of double sessions. He scheduled a controlled scrimmage four days after the team's arrival in Raleigh. Interestingly, Schwartzwalder looked upon Bowl games as a reward to the players for a job well done. He always took the entire team to Bowl games, not just the thirty-five players who made up the travel squad during the regular season. Syracuse was fortunate that no serious injuries occurred during the two scrimmages, but many players had minor bumps and bruises as they headed for Miami.

DICK EASTERLY (Quarterback): "A lot of people don't recall

that we did have a separate squad which practiced as the Oklahoma team down in North Carolina. I really look at it as the heart of the foundation of the '59 team. You know that 1958 football team had to be very good to get there. Heck, they were playing Oklahoma in the Orange Bowl, so there were quite a few good ball players, plus five or six guys that would be starters on our '59 team. Anyway, this practice team, which was supposed to be Oklahoma, was one of the best teams I was ever on. It was made up of third—and fourth-string players as well as us 'redshirts' who were being held out of games that year. Dave Sarette was the quarterback. John Brown, who was a hell of a player and later went on to the NFL, played one of the two tackle positions. Leon Cholokis, who made some big plays in 1959, was on our line, as was big Gene Grabowsky, who came over from Penn State and was also redshirting. A lot of guys on that team went on to play a lot of football at Syracuse over the next three years. We also had a great leader in Dickie Beyer. If anyone could inspire anyone, this guy could. He would get us over there on the practice field alone and beat us up, yelling and screaming, getting us fired up. He actually got us believing we were the individual ball players that played for Oklahoma. We would practice separately, particularly during the couple of days before the scrimmages. We had our own jerseys and we had our own helmets. We really became the Oklahoma team and, for those two or three days, we believed it. During the opening scrimmage—which had officials calling penalties—we got the ball because there were no kickoffs. I think the second play of the scrimmage, Pat Caramanna, who never did play a lot of ball in 1959, broke one for about 78 yards for a touch-down. The next series after we scored we held the first group from scoring. We got the ball back and I was playing halfback and I broke one for 60 yards and a touchdown. We had scored six times while the group that was going to play in the Orange Bowl had not scored any. Ben got mad and called the scrimmage off. He was quite frustrated. I don't know if he thought at that point, because he was getting ready for the Orange Bowl,'Hey I wonder if these guys are going to be this good next year?' I think three days went by and we had another scrim-mage. Pretty much the same thing happened and I remember Dick Beyer said, 'Don't lay off these guys because you're getting them ready

Dick Beyer with a game face. Courtesy of Dick Beyer.

for the Orange Bowl.' We were fired up. The first team had the ball and they were moving down the field but then they fumbled and we recovered. We got the ball and we went down the field and scored. We scored two more times and the first team had not scored yet. Ben was furious. He actually tore into Dick Beyer.'If I didn't have to redshirt those guys, I'd start the lot of them. I know they could move the ball against Oklahoma.' Boy, he was mad."

JOHN BROWN (Tackle): "I was one of the 'greenies (fourth team).' I was redshirted that year. He took all of us down there for the Orange Bowl practices. I remember Ben told me afterwards, 'Hey, you continue working like that you should be able to play.' I needed that for my confidence."

LEON CHOLOKIS (Tackle): "I remember Jimmy Wright during those practices in North Carolina. Ben would come in and give us a pep talk. We would be on offense near our own goal line practicing against the first group. This wasn't the scrimmage but one of the practices. Anyway, Ben would come in and he would say to Jimmy, or to whomever was quarterback, 'Call a play so we can defend against it and don't tell me. Call anything you want.' Well, Jimmy called for a quick kick. Ben went ballistic. He came in and reamed out all of us, not just Jimmy. It was very funny though."

Oklahoma on the other hand took a completely different approach to their practices. Concentrating on conditioning and polishing their intricate offensive plays, Wilkerson's main concern was making sure his team's offense was run with precision. The Syracuse staff inwardly referred to the Sooners offense as the "garbage offense" because of the unorthodox sets Oklahoma used moving players all over the field in an effort to confuse the opponent.

The exceptional team speed of the Sooners had made them a solid 13-point favorite in the game. The Oklahoma head coach felt his team's advantage would be speed and quickness, but more importantly, being prepared to offset Syracuse's physical play. The Syracuse players were confident going into the game, as no team had run over the Orange the entire season.

On January 1, 1959, 75,281 fans jammed into the old Miami stadium to watch the 25th edition of the Orange Bowl. Oklahoma won the toss, and with their first unit looking crisp, moved the ball down the field for the game's first score, a nifty 42-yard run by left halfback Prentiss Gault. Syracuse, not to be denied, took the ensuing kickoff and marched down the field. Gambling on fourth down from the Oklahoma 45-yard line, the Orangemen faked a punt and quarterback Chuck Zimmerman hit left end Dave Baker with a perfect pass to give Syracuse a first down at the Oklahoma 25-yard line. On the next play, halfback Tom Stephens stumbled forward to the Oklahoma 20-yard line, was hit, fumbled, and the Sooners recovered. Two plays later Oklahoma stung Syracuse with a 79-yard touchdown pass. Right halfback Brewster Hobby rolled left and tossed a short pass to left end Ross Coyle who went the distance untouched. Oklahoma was up, 14–0.

Syracuse never recovered and lost, 21–6. Oklahoma's team speed, well advertised prior to the game, totally dominated Syracuse. The players were rocked by the quick scores and lost their poise. Backs bumping into backs and stupid penalties continued to plague Syracuse all game long. The players never quit, but the aggressive style of play that carried this team all year was not present. Midway through the third quarter Syracuse had marched to midfield and faced a fourth-and-one. Ordinarily, Schwartzwalder, trusting his big physical line, would go for the first down. Instead, Syracuse punted. The coaches and the players were totally out of sync. Toward the end of the game, trailing by fifteen points, the Orangemen's offense needed to move quickly. Instead they were methodical. Oklahoma's eleven starters had clearly outplayed Syracuse's first group.

Following the game, Schwartzwalder came under considerable fire from both the media and fans alike for his team's poor performance. It wasn't so much the 21–6 drubbing they got but rather the perceived lack of aggressiveness and Ben's conservative play calling. Schwartz-walder, who was now 0–3 in Bowl games, looked far from the coach capable of making the Orange a legitimate national power. He knew changes had to be made. His team needed to get quicker, adding more speed at the skill positions. The Orangemen would have a wealth of talent returning next year, including last season's redshirts and an outstanding sophomore class led by a young kid named Ernie Davis. Expectations would once again be high. Syracuse fans were tired of seeing their Orangemen beat up other Eastern teams only to be outclassed in Bowl games. They wanted a team that could do more. They wanted a national power. They wanted to win a Bowl game against a quality team. The pressure was definitely on to get to the next level.

MAURY YOUMANS (Tackle): "When we arrived in North Carolina in preparation for the Orange Bowl the shocking thing to me was there was snow on the ground. We get off the bus and there's snow on the ground. Here we were leaving Syracuse where there was a lot of snow and we get to this place and there's still snow. I thought this is kind of crazy. What are we coming here for if there is going to be snow on the ground? Well, it didn't last that long, so we ended up practicing, but it was still cold. I just felt that going into a game like the Orange Bowl, where it was really basically warm, we could have gone to some place that might have been warmer. Schwartzwalder didn't want to arrive in Florida too early because of his perceived distractions that Miami had to offer. He felt it contributed to his team's poor play in the 1953 Orange Bowl. I remember Ben said, 'I'm not going to make the same mistake that we made coming down here in playing in the Orange Bowl. They had us doing everything. We were in every parade. Whatever special event there was, we were in it.' Ben cut us right out of that stuff."

GERHARD SCHWEDES (Halfback): "During the Orange Bowl game the year before Ben point-blank panicked. He had the wrong guys in during the game at the wrong times. He got it all screwed up. After that game, going into my senior season, he and I talked about it. He asked me, 'Do you know where we went wrong playing against Oklahoma?' I never told him that he blew the game on his decisions. But I told him, 'Coach, you overworked us.' By the time we got to the Orange Bowl we were absolutely pooped. We were done. If he had a fault, and he had a few, he'd practiced us too long. I mean he ran us into the ground. He was so intense he just worked us to death. After that, he and I had an agreement. He said, 'If you ever feel that we're at a point where we're overworking the team, just give me a signal and we'll end practice.' He had no idea how hard he worked his teams. He was just so engrossed in what he was doing. He never understood that."

ROGER DAVIS (Guard): "Oklahoma beat the crap out of us. They had a heck of a team. We weren't quite ready yet."

Dave SARETTE

QUARTERBACK

My freshman year I remember we were the scout team for the Iowa State game. Damned if Iowa State didn't run a single wing, so that automatically made me the single wing tailback. I was an 'under the center quarterback,' not a single wing tailback. I can remember the varsity is out there in their defense. The coaches had this cardboard, which had written on it, all the Iowa State plays. These were the plays, the scout team was to run. They said, 'Let's run an off tackle play.' I took the snap and ran off-tackle. Son of a gun, I run through the line, and before I'm tackled, I cut back quickly, and I ended up running for a touchdown. On the very first play, I'm coming back, and there were some comments made from the varsity players. Things like, 'You ain't doing that shit again.' We're going to get you! Who the hell do you think you are?' Schwartzwalder comes back to the huddle, and he's upset because I broke it for a touchdown. He comes back and says,'Same play.' I said, 'Oh shit!' I made sure I ran into somebody really quick like, and fell down.

"I was on a highly touted freshman team as far as recruitment was concerned. The coaches knew they had some good players on that team. We had John Brown, we had Dick Easterly, and we had Art Baker. We had a few other guys that would play a lot of football at Syracuse, like Bobby Stem, Tom Gilburg and Bruce Tarbox. Tarbox didn't play as much his freshman year, but that's why they called him, 'The Cinderella Kid.' When he came back his sophomore year he was so much bigger. We had a really good team.

"Our first game we played Cornell and we whipped them easily. We then went down to Army and whipped them. We were doing very well and I was having a good year. Our last game we were scheduled to play Colgate at home. I was by then being touted as a pretty good quarterback by the coaches. I was playing so well they made me captain of the team. The freshmen game against Colgate, that field was just lined with alumni all over. Well in that game I throw seven interceptions, seven interceptions! That was the last game of the season and obviously now I'm at the lowest point of my life. No coaches talk to me the rest of the year. We come to my sophomore year and I was told right off that I would be redshirted. The quarterbacks were Chuck Zimmerman, Dan Fogarty, and Bobby Thomas. I remember players used to go into the coach's office and you kind of sneak a look at the depth charts. Well, I was not even on the depth chart. That's how low I was. They were redshirting me because they didn't know what else to do with me. I was given a locker so far away from everybody that you know you're on your own. I just sat there and said, 'Well I've either got to quit or I got to do something.' I said I'm not going to quit so I just got to find out where I'm going to play. I could have transferred at that point but it was the pride factor. I knew my ability and I knew that I had to seek an opportunity. I knew that I was better than anybody I saw out there, I just needed to have a chance.

"Practice starts and they gave me a green shirt, and by the way, Easterly got one too.(Note: Green practice jerseys were worn by the fourth team.) There were a few others on the team that also got them. That year we were the defense for the scout team. I did not get under the center for the whole year. I'm a sophomore now, that's how bad they looked at me. They based everything on that one game, even though I had played well in the other games. Bill Bell wouldn't give me a shot. I was not one of his favorites at that time.

"We were the green team the whole year, just getting beat up. We'd come to a practice and they'd put us on defense. What got me is that they would run live offensive plays against us instead of using dummies. I'm sure it was just to discourage us. 'You know we aren't going to use you, so leave or something,' because I got a full scholarship. I'm sure they wanted to get it back somehow. Anyway, I can remember playing defensive linebacker on the green team and having to hit Ernie Davis who was a freshman at that time. I hit him and I thought my shoulder was going to fall off. I got back in there and all I did was pray that whole scrimmage that Ernie wouldn't come back my way.

"The key to me finally getting a break that year was Pat Stark, the quarterback coach. Pat Stark, for some reason, and Dick Beyer took a liking to me. I can remember telling Dick Beyer, somehow I want to play. If I can't be a quarterback, I got to be something, I got to play. So Beyer said,'Well, maybe you're just not tough enough.' I said, 'I'll go one-on-one with any of your players.' So I did go one-on-one, with one of the players. I can picture the guy. He was a third string tackle. We went one-on-one, and after that was over, Beyer had some respect for me.

"Pat Stark always felt I could throw the ball well. He would see me pass the ball on my own. When we were going down for the Orange Bowl in January of '59 he picked me to run Oklahoma's offense. I had never been under center the whole year but he picked me over some other guys. Being put on that team, I think, was the best thing that ever happened to me. We were in North Carolina and we were running Oklahoma's plays. We started out running them against the first team, and honestly, we beat the hell out of them. Then we played the second team, and we beat them. Then they even put in a third team, and we beat them. Schwartzwalder was livid. We were supposed to fly into Miami the next day and he cancelled it. He says, 'We're going to scrimmage one more time.' So we went out there again with the same results. That week brought me back as a contender for next year's quarterback position. Otherwise I doubt they would have even consider me."

Bill RAPP, Jr.

STUDENT MANAGER,'59

I was student manager in 1959 and we were in the locker room getting ready for the Kansas game. A coach tapped me on the shoulder and he says, 'Take these tickets up by Archbold Gym and see what you can get for them.' He then adds, 'See if you can get around forty dollars for them.' I had heard recently that there had been an article in the newspaper about the fact that they were going to be watching for people scalping tickets. Here I am a little freshman and I wasn't about to tell him no. So up I go and I'm not sure exactly how to do it, or what to do. At that time I believe the tickets are probably worth around seven dollars each. He had four tickets. I knew that there were people milling around up there and I probably could sell them. Also, you could see that there were some tickets being exchanged. So this guy comes up to me and says, 'What do you want for them?' I said, 'I have these excellent tickets, four of them on the forty yard line.' He then says, 'Let's go into the men's room.' I thought, THE MEN'S ROOM! I didn't know if this guy was a molester or what, but I went on in. Low and behold, as he's reaching for his wallet, this big hand hits me on the shoulder, and it's one of Syracuse's finest. I said, 'Well look, I'm a student manager, and I'm just trying to . . . .' In fact, I think I introduced myself. The cop says, 'Your grandfather was the Chief of Police in Syracuse. What are you doing scalping tickets?' Anyway, the policeman said. 'Look, do what you got to do. Just go around the corner and get it done.' I got a touch short of forty dollars, but I took it back to the coach. I never heard anything about it again. In fact he never asked me to do it again. I guess he thought I wasn't a good enough bargainer."

Ben Schwartzwalder. Courtesy of Syracuse University Archives.

Coach

"Good fellows are a dime a dozen but an aggressive leader is priceless."
—Red Blaik
Former Head Coach of Army

In the pre-dawn hours of June 6, 1944, troops of G Company, 507th Parachute Infantry, 82nd Airborne Division, were headed for France. They were preparing to jump into a part of history. Most of the young paratroopers quietly stared into space, lips tight, perspiration across their brow, hoping for the best, fearing the worst. Many prayed. Others broke the tension by scribbling letters home knowing they may never be mailed.

Toward the back of the plane two young men, boys really, softly carried on a conversation about what each would do when the war was over. The greatest invasion of all time would have many casualties, and the men of the 507th knew some of them would not make it out alive. One soldier though was different from the others. Captain Ben Schwartzwalder, sitting up front next to the exit, was sound asleep. Schwartzwalder had spent the entire night making sure his men would be ready for the jump. His experiences before the war as a college athlete and coach had taught him the importance of detail. Leaving nothing to chance, he checked each man's parachute, making sure they had been packed properly. With the soldiers of G Company, he reviewed their objectives once they were safely on the ground. Looking each man in the eye he reassured them that they were ready. They had trained hard, and as long as they focused on the job at hand, they would be fine. It was time to do their duty. He knew that he was ready and he felt his men were ready too. It was time to go to war.

Floyd Burdette Schwartzwalder grew up in Huntington, West Virginia. His brothers had nicknamed him Ben when he was six years old and the name had stuck throughout his lifetime. Early in life his father had taught his three sons the value of hard work. His father. an immigrant from Germany, operated a nursery and landscaping business. He was by all accounts a task master. A part-time preacher, he had little tolerance for sports, and he would tell his three sons, "You want exercise, pick up a shovel and do some work." Young Ben contracted influenza when he was ten years old. The only food his body could handle was pears, and for over a month, that was the only thing he could eat. As a consequence of eating poorly he grew up to be a skinny kid. One day while reading a comic book he saw an advertisement on bodybuilding. The next day he sent away for a 'Stretcher' and began to strengthen his body. Schwartzwalder became hooked on strength-training and quickly built up his body. Ben's two older brothers secretly played sports, never daring to let their father know.

One afternoon while Ben was playing football at school, his father came by unexpectedly. Rather than expel his son from the game, Mr. Schwartzwalder observed the action and slowly realized that sports "Wasn't so bad after all." Shortly thereafter Ben's father attended all of his games, cheering on 'My son.' The father's influence on his youngest son was great. A short, stocky man, he remained a man of vigor his entire lifetime. When he was fifty-seven years old, the truck he was driving went off a road, landing in a rock pile at the bottom of a ravine. It was estimated that he was unconscious for approximately six hours. When he finally came to, he crawled on his hands and knees to a nearby home where the people called for help.

BEN SCHWARTZWALDER: "When they brought him home the doctor knew he had no chance of making it. For a whole month, lying in bed, he talked to me, telling me what he expected of me. 'Work hard,' he told me. 'Better yourself. Whatever you do, do it the best you can.' I've never forgotten that. Finally, when he went into his death throes, I couldn't stay awake any longer. I knew, while falling asleep, that when I awoke, my father would be dead. And that's the way it was."

Besides football in high school, Ben tried his hand at basketball but it wasn't for him. He thought it too passive a game and so he went out for wrestling instead. He excelled in wrestling. Schwartzwalder felt that wrestling helped him with his agility and quickness, which in turn made him a better football player. All of this contributed to his making All-State at center his senior year. The University of Pittsburgh showed an interest in Schwartzwalder and came to Huntington to visit. When Ben got on the scales and weighed only 148 pounds they lost interest. His high school coach had arranged for him to go to Purdue but Ben wanted to attend West Virginia. Unfortunately, like Pittsburgh, the West Virginia coaching staff felt he was too small for college football. Ben was furious. West Virginia had just signed a player he had played against in high school who Ben thought wasn't very good. He decided to attend West Virginia's football camp and show them first hand what they would be missing. He got his scholarship!

At West Virginia he was the toughest player on the team. His coach, Earle "Greasy" Neal, loved him. Running the single-wing offense, the center was a key component in the blocking scheme and Schwartzwalder did it well. He was a tenacious blocker on offense and a fierce tackler on defense. He was so admired by the coaches and other players for his toughness and dedication that he was chosen to captain the team during his junior and senior years.

During his freshman year he met a girl named Reggie, the girl who would become his partner for life.

REGGIE SCHWARTZWALDER: "We were married right after we graduated in 1933. We had met at West Virginia. I was from a little town in West Virginia called Pine Grove. Ben was from Huntington. I met Ben the first day I was at the University. We had freshman orientation and I saw him come into the room. He was coming in from foot-

Young Ben in his West Virginia letter sweater.
Courtesy of Reggie Schwartzwalder.

ball practice and he had a patch over his eye . . . and that's how I remember him. We started dating shortly after that."

The director of health and physical education at West Virginia at
that time, Dr. Carl P. Schott, became very interested in Ben. Dr.
Schott's door was always open to him, and over the next four years at
West Virginia, they became close friends, so close that after graduation
it was Dr. Schott who recommended Ben for his first coaching job at
Sisters High School in his native West Virginia. The job didn't last

Mrs. Ben Schwartzwalder (Reggie).
Courtesy of Reggie Schwartzwalder.

long. Coaching at a small school his first year, he was discouraged when only thirteen kids came out for football. Getting beat 48–0 in his first game against Benwood Union, one player even refused to go in. Things went from bad to worse, and following the season, Ben got fired.

After serving a year as an assistant coach at Wenton High, Schwartzwalder, through Dr. Schott's efforts, was hired as head football coach at Parkersburg High School. This time he had a nucleus of players. In 1938 and 1940, his team won state titles. The next year he moved onto Canton-McKinley high school in Canton, Ohio. Dr. Schott convinced Ben that he had it too easy at Parkersburg. He said if coaching football is all he wanted to do, changing jobs would be necessary for him to continue to grow as a coach. Ben agreed. That December, the United States went to war, and Ben Schwartzwalder resigned his position as football coach. In the spring of 1942, he enlisted into the army.

Reggie Schwartzwalder: "Dr. Schott was Dean of Physical Education and Athletics at West Virginia when we were in school there. He was always like a father to Ben over the years. Whenever Ben made a choice of moving out or moving on, he would confer with Dr. Schott. He always recommended Ben for coaching jobs, including Syracuse. We kept in touch with him our whole lives."

Ben Schwartzwalder was in the Reserve Officer Training Corp Program (ROTC) at West Virginia. He entered the army as a Captain and was sent to Fort Benning, Georgia for basic training. Next he was sent to Camp Croft in South Carolina for parachute infantry training. The training was hard. The soldiers awoke at four-thirty in the morning, beginning each day with a six mile run, followed by brisk callisthenics. After breakfast they had inspection and then he had to attend classes throughout the rest of the day. Schwartzwalder thrived in this environment. Always in great shape, he loved the discipline of the army and the challenges of jump school. The days were long and only the toughest made it through.

When jump school was completed Ben was assigned to the 507th. Initially stationed in Nebraska, the 507th was sent back to Georgia prior to being deployed to northern Ireland in December of 1943. In March, 1944, they were sent to Nottingham, England to prepare for Operation Overlord, better known as D-Day.

REGGIE SCHWARTZWALDER: "Ben had participated in the ROTC program while at West Virginia. He went into the Army, I believe as a captain. His first active duty was in 1942 at Fort Benning in Georgia. From there he went to Camp Croft in South Carolina and that's when he went into the parachute troops. He was older than most of the boys that went through that training, but he was an officer, so that was all right, I guess. Once the parachute training was over, they were shipped off to Nebraska. They were training to go to Africa in desert type conditions. Apparently Nebraska had an area that was desert-like. He ended up going back to Fort Benning before his orders were changed and was then sent to Ireland instead of Africa."

D-Day had been planned for many months. The Normandy Invasion was to go deep inside German-occupied France, and if successful, effectively destroy any chances Germany had of winning the war. The 507th Parachute Infantry's objective in the invasion was to secure a western crossing area, near the Village of Cauquigny, on the west bank of the Meredet River. While the 507th was securing its position, other

Ben and Reggie the night before he went to war. Courtesy of Reggie Schwartzwalder.

regiments of the 82nd Airborne (505th, 508th) would be securing the eastern and the southwestern end of the drop zone, respectively. Once these areas were captured, the allied ground forces with their flanks now being protected could begin moving into the area. Unfortunately, things did not go according to plan. Aerial maps of the area failed to properly identify the marshes located in the drop zone. In addition, the Germans flooded the area. Tall grasses growing in clusters camouflaged the water. Many of the unsuspecting soldiers, landing in water four-feet deep, were dragged down by their heavy equipment and drowned.

Besides men, important radio equipment was lost, making communication between the troops nonexistent. Facing Germany's tough Seventh Army, the soldiers also had to deal with the difficult terrain which consisted of century-old hedgerows, thorny bushes, and trees. Captain Schwartzwalder, lying in the darkened field and unsure of where the enemy was, could hear the splashing of men desperately trying to rid themselves of the parachutes and equipment which was slowly pulling them down into a watery grave. Not knowing any other objective but G Company's, Schwartzwalder, with a few of his men, headed west to find the rest of the regiment and re-group. Once located, Schwartzwalder's platoon was chosen to take control of the LaFiere Bridge.

BEN SCHWARTZWALDER: "The next morning I walked over to where three Americans were talking. One of them had those stars on, and it was Ridgeway (General Matthew Ridgeway, Commander of the 82nd Airborne Division) talking to a Colonel. He said, 'I want that damned bridge.' The Colonel looked around and saw me, and said, 'Captain we want that bridge.' I looked around and there was nobody else, so I was stuck with it."

That evening G Company, led by Ben Schwartzwalder, approached the LaFiere Bridge. When G Company moved within a thousand yards of the bridge they were pinned down by German machine gun fire. The first attempt at wiping out the machine gun failed and the men were forced to retreat. Schwartzwalder reorganized his men, and inching closer in the darkness through the dense thicket, they were able to take out the German machine gun. Schwartzwalder's men could now move within five hundred yards of their target which enabled them to overrun the remaining Germans and seize the bridge. For twelve hours they were pounded by the Germans but they never surrendered that bridge. G Company, besides securing the LaFiere Bridge, a strategic crossing for the invasion, killed twenty of the enemy and captured ten others. Schwartzwalder was awarded the Silver Star.

The next time he saw Ridgeway, the General looked at him and said, "Captain, I never thought I would see you again." (Ben noted later, "I was impressed he remembered me.")

GENERAL MARSHALL (Chief Historian, European Theater of Operations): "Mortar fire was coming from somewhere on the other side of the river. Before it had quieted, Schwartzwalder was bound for the other side. This man loves a fight."

The war didn't stop here for Schwartzwalder and the rest of the 507th. Their next objective was to secure the Cotentin Peninsula. In the ensuing thirty-three days the 507th would be in some of the most vicious fighting of the war. In mid July 1944 the battered, but highly respected members of the 507th, were sent back to England for some much needed rest.

In August of 1944 the battle-tested 507th, was assigned to the 17th Airborne Division which was training and in need of a parachute division. That December the 507th participated in the Battle of the Bulge and led the assault on Luxembourg. The 17th Airborne continued its push forward, and in late March 1945, the 507th parachuted deep into Germany territory. In a spectacular night drop, they landed three miles from the Town of Wesel. The battle was over in four and a half hours. The American army battered the German forces into submission and secured the town. The American troops continued to push forward, and on April 10, 1945, captured the town of Essen, the home of the Krupp steel factory. Less than a month later the Germans surrendered. In September 1945, Ben and the rest of the 507th finally shipped home.

Ben Schwartzwalder by all accounts, was an outstanding soldier. Brave, a natural born leader of men, he participated in three major offenses, won a Presidential Citation, the Silver and Bronze Stars, and was given the Purple Heart for being wounded during the Battle Of the Bulge. Schwartzwalder never openly discussed his war experiences. He, like so many of his generation, felt it belittled those who had paid the ultimate sacrifice and did not make it back home.

A national writer came to Syracuse following the 1959 season to do a story on Schwartzwalder. During the interview, Ben sat at his desk, head down, doodling plays, answering questions, not being very talkative. In an attempt to get him to open up more, the writer mentioned that he had heard that the old coach was a war hero. Schwartzwalder set down his pen, took off his glasses, glared up at the writer and said, "Who told you that?" And then added, "What the hell does that have to do with football?" The writer got the point and moved onto a very frosty interview.

Following the war, Dr. Schott had heard that Muhlenberg College in Allentown, Pennsylvania was looking for a football coach and recommended Ben. After two interviews, Schwartzwalder was chosen as the new coach. He compiled a record of twenty-five wins and five losses in three years at that Pennsylvania school. Those years were spent refining his coaching skills. Initially, a proponent of the single-wing, Schwartzwalder now was moving his quarterback under center and running a straight "T" offense with the three backs lining up behind the quarterback. He incorporated some changes, kept parts of the single wing that he liked, and merged them into his own offensive schemes. He tinkered with using an unbalanced line, trying to set up mismatches along the scrimmage line. He continued to develop his power football with two-on-one blocking. He preferred his quarterbacks handling the ball as long as possible, running the option play to complement his 'Belly' or 'Ride' series. The halfback pass was implemented into his offense to keep the defense honest. His total dedication to the game of football drove him to constantly learn and try new things. He wasn't content to just follow what the other coaches were doing. He wanted to create his own style. He was totally consumed by the game of football. It would remain that way for the rest of his life.

JIM SHREVE (Freshmen Coach): "It was interesting when we would go to clinics and he would lecture on the unbalanced line. He was ahead of his time in developing things, and because it was complicated to learn, he would totally lose those guys taking notes. Everyone was running balanced lines in those days, and these young, high school coaches would get lost trying to understand the intricacies of his offense. It was so complicated they could not get the notes down by the time the lecture ended. I went to a lot of clinics and coached thirty years in six different schools but no one ever duplicated his offense because it was so damned advanced."

Early one morning in the spring of 1949, Dr. Scott called once more, telling the young coach he was going to Syracuse.

"What?" Ben protested. "Syracuse and Ohio State are the two graveyards of coaching." Dr. Schott assured him that he was the right man for the job. The next day he gathered up all his information, including game film of his team, and headed for the Warrick Hotel in Philadelphia to meet with Syracuse Athletic Director, Lew Andreas.

Andreas was on a mission to find a new coach. The Syracuse football program was in a shambles. The 1948 team, under the tutelage of Reaves "Ribs" Baysinger, had gone 1–8 for the season, beating Niagara in the opener and then losing eight straight games. Syracuse hadn't had a winning season since before the war, in 1942. Baysinger could have salvaged his job if he had agreed to replace all of his staff. He declined, and was promptly fired. Twelve coaches had applied for the open position but Andreas was so impressed with Schwartzwalder, especially because he was the only coach who brought his game film, that he recommended Ben the very next day to the athletic board.

Schwartzwalder was approved by the Board and all that was needed was the approval by the Chancellor, William P. Tolley. Tolley, a Syracuse alumnus, had roomed at Syracuse with legendary college coach Lynn "Pappy" Waldorf. Although an educator first, the Syracuse chancellor understood the importance of athletics. He interviewed Schwartzwalder over the telephone and quickly determined Ben was the man for the job. Ben accepted a three-year contract at $8,500 dollars per year and became the twenty-third coach in Syracuse football history.

Schwartzwalder was not a popular choice in the Syracuse fans' eyes. They were expecting a "name coach" to be hired. Instead they got some "no-name" guy from a small school in Pennsylvania.

BEN SCHWARTZWALDER: "The alumni wanted a big-name coach, instead. They got a long named coach."

The following Monday, after being hired as head coach, Schwartzwalder had his team practicing. Of his hastily assembled staff, only Roy Simmons was kept from the old regime. Simmons, a legendary figure in Syracuse University sports, had been All America in lacrosse, and captain and quarterback on the 1924 football team. He was instrumental in bringing the new coach up to speed on personnel and opponents. They began putting together a plan to recruit players. A major problem was that the administration allowed only twelve scholarships per class. In comparison, Big Ten schools and other national powers during that same period had twice as many grants-in-aid to build their football teams. Nonetheless, Schwartzwalder and his staff persevered.

When the new coach arrived on the hill, the freshman football coach had handled ninety percent of the recruiting. That changed immediately. Ben divided up territories for his staff to cover but he would go wherever he was needed. Each year they would screen more than five thousand high school and prep school players.

The team won four games that first year, five games each of the next two years, and in 1952 went 7–2, winning the Eastern Crown and a trip to the Orange Bowl. There were no more losing seasons leading up to 1959.

As the schedule continued to get tougher, Schwartzwalder complained about the lack of scholarships offered each year by Syracuse.

BEN SCHWARTZWALDER: "Following the 1949 season when we went 4–5, I complained everywhere. Finally the Chancellor got wind of it and called me in and gave me a good bawling out. But they were doing so little for football, ole Ben was desperate."

JIM SHREVE (Freshmen Coach): "I went in the service in 1945. When I came back, Baysinger had gotten fired and Ben was coming in. I was a player on that first team Ben coached at Syracuse. I'll never forget the first meeting we had in old Archbold, upstairs. He had an assistant by the name of Bud Barker who was really a great guy and a great coach. He was a terrific recruiter. He had come with Ben from Muhlenberg. Bud was smoking a cigarette during the meeting. Ben walked over and took it right out of his mouth and started smoking it right in front of us. I couldn't believe it. Of course back then smoking was acceptable. It was weird, but it was showing his aggressiveness, just taking charge. In those days, when you recruited, you brought prospects in who actually suited up and scrimmaged against the varsity. That was amazing. He brought in a ton of guys that next year. I remember every Saturday during spring practice we would have these recruits out there in full pads."

REGGIE SCHWARTZWALDER: "Coming to Syracuse in 1949 was quite a bit different then it is now, shall we say. I don't think they had very many scholarships, maybe twelve. I don't even think that many. But the team played both ways then, so maybe they didn't need so many. It was rough that first year because he just took what he had, you know. I remember that Ted Dailey came with him. Ted was coaching at a high school in Pennsylvania and he already knew Ted. They had played against each other in college. Ted played at Pittsburgh. Ben always claimed that when West Virginia played Pittsburgh, that Ted broke his leg. Somebody broke his leg in that game and he always said it was Ted. That made the story better I guess, and maybe it was Ted, I don't know. Anyway, he got him right away, when he knew he could bring someone with him. Bill Bell was a player at Muhlenberg and came as a graduate assistant, which turned into a full-time job. Ben had a boy named Clyde Barker—we called him Bud—who came with him from Muhlenberg to coach the line. He later went back into the Air Force so it left a vacancy and he went after Rocco Pirro right away. Rock came maybe one or two years later."

JIM SHREVE (Freshmen Coach): "I got married before my last season in 1950. I was living in the trailer camp out by Drumlins. We had a hurricane, and you know Ben didn't call off practice. You couldn't get out and around, but we had practice. I, like an idiot, I was so conscientious, I was one of the guys that went to practice. There weren't many there, but it was in the middle of a hurricane, and he's practicing."

The success of the football program from 1952 forward, and two major Bowl appearances, helped Syracuse's recruiting tremendously. Still, Schwartzwalder was limited in his overall recruiting budget compared to the other schools Syracuse competed against. Consequently, Syracuse recruited almost exclusively within the east, going as far south as Maryland, and as far west as Ohio. Pennsylvania, New England, New Jersey and New York were recruited heavily. Ben complained to the athletic director that he and his staff had to drive their beat-up old cars in order to visit recruits. Soon after, one new station wagon was provided for their use. The administration wanted a good football program, but were reluctant to provide Schwartzwalder the budget to compete on even ground with the other elite football programs.

Dick BEYER

ASSISTANT COACH

I was chosen as Athlete of the Year in 1953 by the New York Alumni Club. Ben and I got on a train to go to New York City to accept the award. We got on the train and we drew x's and o's all the way to New York and all the way back. I'm a graduating senior and I said, 'I'm really not interested in x's and o's.' That didn't matter to Ben because that's the way he was. If you talk to his wife, hell even his dog, football came first, the dog came second, and poor Reggie was last. He was absorbed!

"I was a graduate assistant at Syracuse in 1953. Ben hired me to the staff full-time in 1954. Once the season was over I went to Columbus, Ohio to wrestle professionally. Well, when I came back for the 1955 season, Ben says, 'We got a problem. The Chancellor says we can't have Dick Beyer wrestling professionally and being a football coach at Syracuse at the same time. It doesn't look right.' Ben says, 'The Chancellor has a bug up his ass about a write up in the newspaper.' There had been a riot at a wrestling match where some people got hurt. He says, 'We can't let you coach this year.' So I go to Chicago and become Rookie of the Year in Pro Wrestling. I was there in September, October, November and December. Then I got booked in Hawaii. Anyway, I get a call out there from Ben. He says, 'We got to have you back.' The

28

reason was is that I had proctored in the dorm. I made sure the guys studied every night and went to classes. The two years before that I had done that, everybody passed. The year I wasn't there, they lost about ten guys because there wasn't somebody like me to stay on them. The Chancellor relented. I was allowed to come back and coach football *and* wrestle professionally."

Dick EASTERLY

QUARTERBACK

One night it was snowing and cold. A bunch of us were out and my ex-brother-in-law Johnny Howell, heck of a ball player, got into a little tussle with a couple of guys from Herkimer, or some place. He went outside to fight the guy. In those days that's what you did. You went outside and started swinging at each other. Anyway, I'm standing there with a friend of mine, Frank Mambuca, and a few other guys. Howell hits the guy a couple of times, the guy whacks him back. All of a sudden, John goes down on the ground and hits his head on the sidewalk. The guy starts to beat on him. I was always taught that you have to come to defend your guys. I grabbed the guy off of him and his brother swung at me. Well, the next thing I know I was fighting with him. Mambuca was taking care of the other guy. To make a long story short, we won the battle and these guys were beat up. The next day I got called into Ben's office. Boy, was I nervous. Ben says to me, 'Easterly, I heard that you got in a big tussle last night.' Now he's dead serious and he says, 'We're going to be talking about maybe losing a scholarship here unless you answer the question right.' And his question was, 'Did you lick em?' I told him I had won, and he said, 'Case dismissed.' That was the end of it. That's how Ben was."

Dick Easterly. Courtesy of Syracuse University Athletic Communications.

Bob Thomas. Courtesy of Syracuse University Sports Information.

3

"Hey! Who's Playing Quarterback?"

The team as a whole reported to camp in great shape to begin two-a-day practices in preparation for the upcoming season. "Most of the boys look to be in very good shape," commented Schwartzwalder on reviewing the squad. "I don't think we have too many fat men." Everyone was ready to go with the exception of Roger Davis, Syracuse's preseason All American candidate who reported to camp with a bad case of tonsillitis. Davis was considered by Schwartzwalder to have the potential to be the best lineman to ever play at Syracuse. The senior guard was a hard-hitter who possessed outstanding speed. Recruited as an end out of high school, he was to anchor a line that most people felt was the strength of the team. He was everything Schwartzwalder liked in his lineman . . . big, tough and fast. The entire line, with the exception of tackle Bob Yates, had been recruited either as an end or as a back. All the projected starters were athletic.

Bob Thomas had backed up the backup quarterback for the previous two years. Thomas had a sensational spring practice, demonstrating outstanding passing skills and a true understanding of the Syracuse offensive playbook. Coaches and the media all agreed that with

Thomas at quarterback Syracuse would have another outstanding team, perhaps the best ever. The senior from Edmonston, Maryland had no real competition for the starting job. Two redshirted sophomores, Dave Sarette and local North High School product, Dick Easterly, were already targeted for second and third team positions. Thomas had been experiencing stiffness in his back during the spring, but the training staff felt that with rest over the summer the problem would clear up and he would be ready to play. Ben Schwartzwalder and offensive backfield coach Bill Bell weren't so sure. Thomas was their guy, but with no experience behind him, the coaching staff was nervous. Ben, a master at moving players to different positions where they excelled, needed to develop an insurance plan if Thomas's back did not respond to rest. The question was—Who would that be? Schwartzwalder and Bell decided that the only player capable of making the transition to quarterback would be last year's starting right halfback, Gerhard Schwedes. The 6'1", 191 pound running back from New Jersey who grew up in Germany during World War II, was a leader on the team. Schwedes, not possessing great speed, was a hard worker who responded in games. "He was a darn good football player," Schwartzwalder often said of Schwedes.

GERHARD SCHWEDES (Quarterback): "Bob Thomas got his back hurt in spring practice. He had looked really sharp and everyone felt he could do the job. I knew he had a sore back but I went home for the summer thinking I'm the starting right halfback. Ben called in June and said,'You're going to be the quarterback, start throwing.' I said, 'Coach, I'm not a quarterback!' Ben said, 'Yes you are. You're Syracuse's number one quarterback.' But the funny thing was, I thought I could do it. Ben told me I would be a quarterback until one of the two new kids panned out. Somehow he knew that Thomas wasn't going to be able to play."

DICK EASTERLY (Quarterback): "Going into my first year I had no idea that I was going to be playing quarterback. The year before I had practiced mostly as a running back but I had sort of established myself as a defensive back. When we got to the start of practice in the fall, I think there were eight quarterbacks. They took a picture of all of us but I didn't think I was going to be a quarterback. Hell, they gave me number 49."

On September 5, Coach Schwartzwalder scheduled his team's first scrimmage at Hendrick's field. The team had been going through double sessions for the past four days and it was time to see what they had learned. It was decided that Schwedes would replace Thomas in this scrimmage. Art Baker, Ernie Davis and Mark Weber rounded out the starting backfield. Dave Sarette would quarterback the second unit, with Pete Brokaw, Jim Anderson and Bob Hart as his running mates. Dick Easterly would split time with Jim Saylor as the third team's signal caller.

The staff was eager to see how Schwedes would handle his new position and were equally excited to see Ernie Davis in his first varsity scrimmage. Davis did not disappoint. On his third carry, a simple off-tackle play, Ernie broke through the line, darted to his left, broke two tackles, then scampered 45 yards for a touchdown. To the delight of the coaching staff the young sophomore would break two more plays during the scrimmage. He also caught a short touchdown pass from Schwedes. Schwedes got passing marks for his first effort at quarterback. Overall he ran the offense well although at times his inexperience at quarterback showed. He threw two touchdown passes but was intercepted twice on poorly thrown balls. In contrast, Sarette's play was outstanding. His ball-faking and decision-making were better than Schwedes', and his pinpoint accuracy at passing resulted in two scores.

The first line was made up of Al Bemiller at center, Bruce Tarbox and Otis Godfrey at guard, Maury Youmans and Bob Yates at the tackles, and Dave Baker and Fred Mautino at left and right end, respectively. Roger Davis, still suffering from tonsillitis, had not practiced yet that fall. Although the play was ragged and the backs fumbled often, the coaches inwardly felt it was a good start considering this was only the fifth day of practice. Dick Easterly, who got little opportunity at quarterback, made some outstanding tackles on defense and intercepted one pass. The only casualty for the entire scrimmage was reserve end John Howell who dislocated his finger.

The next day the team, fortified with the return of the projected

Starting backfield (left to right, standing): Ernie Davis, Art Baker, Gerhard Schwedes; (kneeling) Dave Sarette. Courtesy of Syracuse University Sports Information.

starters Bob Thomas and Roger Davis, went back to double sessions. The coaching staff began bearing down on the individual players. Any and all mistakes made during the scrimmage were now being corrected on the practice field. Classes wouldn't begin for a few weeks so it was all football. Football, football, and more football! Six hours a day! And in that hot, merciless sun!

GERHARD SCHWEDES (Quarterback): "Ben's practices were

awful, abusive, and very tough. He would work us to death, two and a half to three hours each practice, nine if you could take it. First you would climb the ropes and then get into the practice. The practices were intense, just yelling and screaming at you all the time. Everything was precise. What I mean is very organized. Every minute was accounted for. I could take it, I'm Germanic, but so could the other guys."

DICK EASTERLY (Quarterback): "After high school I went into the Marines and was sent to Paris Island. I particularly wished I didn't have to go there, but I went. It was difficult but it sort of prepared me a little bit for Ben's practices. I am going to tell you something . . . Paris Island . . . I can't say it was second to Ben's practices but both were tough. Anytime you are out on the field for three hours at a time, and if you make a good play, you might get a little pat on the back, but if you make a bad one, you are going to get screamed at. It was difficult. He made you pay the price and it goes back to being hardnosed, because that's the way Ben was. He did it that way with his troops and it was the same for his players. Those practices were hard . . . there was nothing easy about them."

MAURY YOUMANS (Tackle): "We had very hard practices. First thing we had to do when we left the locker room was climb the ropes. That probably was something he did in the military, training to be a paratrooper. So we climbed the ropes which was almost the equivalent of weight lifting in a way. It developed your arms and shoulders. Then in practice they had a three bag drill. One player would block straight ahead, while the other two players would pull out, simulating a power sweep. Each was required to hit a series of bags before going to the end of the line. We would do it over and over again. Next they had the sled drill. We would hit the seven-man sled and the two-man sled. After that we had this killer drill called the crab. You had to crawl on your hands straight for ten yards, then go backwards for ten yards. Then do the same thing with your stomach facing up. By the time you finished with that you were dead tired. Then we would get into the hitting. After practice we would run a huge lap, followed by running up and down this hill which was adjacent to the practice field. The hill was maybe twenty feet high. Believe me, conditioning was not a problem when we went into a ball game."

LEON CHOLOKIS (Tackle): "Those practices were tough. In one day in the double sessions I lost about twenty-four, twenty-five pounds. But after I drank water I got it all back."

As practice began for the 1959 season fullback Art Baker was the forgotten man. All the talk that fall regarding the backfield was about Ernie Davis and who was going to play quarterback. In 1958 Baker had played fullback behind Ed Kieffer, now gone after inexplicably dropping out of school. Baker, 6'0" and 205 pounds, was an athlete possessed with strength and speed. The previous winter, while wrestling, he had been unbeaten in the regular season and had won the Eastern Heavyweight Championship. Invited to the NCAA Tournament, Baker won the 191-pound title. A native of Erie, Pennsylvania, he was a hard worker, a quiet young man who preferred to let his actions on the field speak for him. The head coach felt Baker could be the top-notch fullback his past teams had lacked. Schwartzwalder, also a wrestler in college, felt Baker had improved his balance through wrestling. Now he was lowering his shoulder when carrying the ball rather than the straight-up approach he had used the year before.

BEN SCHWARTZWALDER (early fall, 1959): "Art could very well be the most underrated player on our team right now. Most of the folks don't know too much about Baker because he played most of the time last year behind Ed Kieffer. But don't kid yourself, Art's got talent. He has both size and speed."

Schwartzwalder, as he approached the '59 season, seriously considered playing three different units in games . . . a first unit that played both offense and defense, a second unit that played just defense and a third unit that played strictly offense.

In 1958 LSU had won the National Championship by utilizing three units. In his first years at LSU, Paul Dietzel, always an innovative coach, had tried to win by playing his eleven best players the majority of the game. Unfortunately, it did not work. Opponents who were using many more players throughout the games eventually wore down the undermanned Tigers. Dietzel realized then that he needed to play more people. In 1958 he decided to develop three units. The first unit consisted of his best athletes and he called them the 'white unit' because they wore white jerseys. Next he put together his second unit that played just offense and called them the 'Go unit.' Lastly he formed a third team that would play just defense. Dietzel decided to refer to this group, as 'The Chinese Bandits.' The name was derived from a character in the well-known comic-strip, "Terry and the Pirates."

Schwartzwalder, because his team appeared on paper to have depth at all positions, was intrigued with the three-platoon system. Unfortunately, Bob Thomas's aching back was prohibiting him from using it. With a healthy Thomas the coach felt he would have six capable halfbacks to utilize the three-platoon system. Without Thomas he would have to move Schwedes to quarterback leaving him only five capable halfbacks. He decided he would have to rethink this three-platoon system. In all his years of coaching he had never seen such competition for positions. It was easy in the early days at Syracuse to complain about a lack of scholarships or a lack of talent but that was not the case this year. The question now was: How do I utilize all these players? For Ben it was an interesting problem . . . the type of problem all coaches wanted to have.

Schwartzwalder and his staff were pushing this group hard. Like during The War, he needed to know who he could depend on in battle. He was not about to back off on the brutality of his preseason practices. He needed to know who could take it and who could not. Regardless of talent or reputation, you had better measure up to his standards of toughness or you simply were not going to play. In his day, as a player, you played whether you were hurt or not. Players went both ways (offense and defense) for as long as you could, with little substitution. He actually played one game with a broken leg. The college game had changed since his playing days in the thirties. And reluctantly he changed right along with it.

Schwartzwalder understood the need to find a balance with this team. He had to make sure in this era of limited-substitution rules that Syracuse had its best unit on the field at all times. Things would fall into place much better if Thomas's ailing back healed. That was a question that needed to be answered quickly.

As it turned out, Bob Thomas's first two days of practice were uneventful and the contact drills he participated in went fine. The young signal-caller would jump right back up after being hit. From here on it seemed he just needed to remain fit to practice each day with the team. No more sitting out. He had to prove to everybody, including himself, that he was healthy and ready to assume the mantel as the number one quarterback. He had three more days to get the rust off before the second full scrimmage.

While the weather stayed hot and humid, the practices remained demanding and players continued to compete hard for positions. Al Bemiller and Dave Applehof were in a close battle for the starting position at center. Mark Weber, a very talented speedster, continued to alternate with the first and second teams depending on whether Schwedes or Thomas was at quarterback. When Thomas worked with the first group, Schwedes lined up at right halfback. When Thomas was out of the lineup, Schwedes played quarterback with Weber moving to the halfback position.

Two of the players who were catching the coaches' eyes during the first days of practice were sophomores Bob Stem and John Brown. Both had been outstanding in the early practices. Stem, a 5'11", 205-pound athlete from Phillipsburg, New Jersey, had been moved from guard to center in spring practice. A tough player, he wasn't expected to be much of a factor his first year on the varsity team, but now he was turning heads with his aggressive play. Big John Brown, from Camden, New Jersey, was another athlete having a terrific preseason. At 6'2", 213 pounds, Brown was blessed with outstanding size and speed. In high school he had run the hundred—yard dash in 10.8 seconds. An all-around athlete, he was All-State in football and All-City in basketball. Redshirted the previous season, the extra year seemed to help the young tackle's play, and he quickly moved to the second team on the depth chart.

The second full-scale scrimmage was held on September 12. It lasted one hour and forty-five minutes. Thomas and Schwedes alternated at quarterback with the first unit. Thomas showed no ill-effects from the contact and played well. His passes were on target and the offense looked sharp with him at quarterback. Schwedes, switching back and forth between quarterback and halfback, completed one pass to Davis for 50 yards and a touchdown. Dave Sarette, again looking good running the second unit, hit Jerry Skonieckzi for three touchdowns.

Alternating with the first and second teams, Weber's play was impressive, breaking off three runs for scores before being injured late in the scrimmage. Another injury of concern was starting left end Dave Baker. He re-injured the knee he had hurt in spring practice. Schwartzwalder was pleased with the overall play and singled out Bob Thomas and Ernie Davis for praise.

BEN SCHWARTZWALDER: "Bob Thomas did an excellent job running the offense. He looks to me to be in fine shape and over his back problems. I thought Ernie Davis played well. He's going to be a good one. He does an awful lot of things well and he really loves to play football. The kids playing defense all admit that he's hard to tackle and he really hits hard. Also, he doesn't take a back seat to anyone playing defense either. He's a complete player."

At the start of the '59 season Syracuse was ranked 20th in the pre-season poll of sportswriters. LSU was an overwhelming choice to repeat as National Champions. With thirty-one lettermen returning from last year's team, including Heisman candidate Billy Cannon, the Tigers looked a solid choice to be the best team in the nation once again. Oklahoma and Auburn were the only other schools given any serious consideration for the top spot. SMU, with senior quarterback Don Meredith, was the favorite to win the Southwest Conference although Texas and TCU were going to have strong teams. As the season approached the Big Ten had four teams ranked in the top ten: Wisconsin, Northwestern, Ohio State and defending league champion, Iowa. Out west, Southern California was the team to beat with UCLA a dark horse candidate. Mississippi looked to be the class team in the Southeastern Conference. Teams mentioned from the east were Penn State and Army. The Cadets were coming off an unbeaten, once-tied season and were led by the All-America end, Bill Carpenter.

Carpenter was nicknamed "The Lonesome End" because he never went into his team's huddle during the entire 1958 season. Fans, as well as coaches, spent the entire year trying to figure out how he received the plays. Years later, Army's coach, Red Blaik claimed that the quarterback, Joe Caldwell, relayed the signals to Carpenter by the movement of his feet.

Besides Carpenter, only three other Eastern players were receiving national attention from the sports media. Penn State's outstanding senior quarterback, Richie Lucas, was the leader on a very good Nittany Lion team. Pittsburgh's junior end, Mike Ditka, and Syracuse's guard, Roger Davis, were being touted as a potential All-America candidates. In general, Eastern football was "Ivy League" . . . fun to watch but not to be considered seriously in the world of college football powers.

On Thursday, September 17, 1959, Bob Thomas and Dave Baker had their season come to an abrupt end. Thomas, who appeared to have gotten through the scrimmage unscathed, woke up that following Sunday morning to a numbing pain in his back. After consulting with the medical staff it became clear that his back problem was not going to go away. Thomas decided it was just too much and decided to forego football for the year.

BOB THOMAS (Quarterback): "What can I say? I've waited two years as a third stringer to get this chance at the varsity level, then this happens."

Dave Baker, Syracuse's most dependable receiver, had been having a very difficult year. First he lost his father, who passed away while watching him play against Oklahoma in the Orange Bowl. Next he hurt his right knee in spring practice. Deciding against surgery, Baker hoped resting the knee over the summer would repair the damage. Unfortunately that did not happen. Baker's loss would be huge. He had proven in his short career to be a clutch receiver for Syracuse. The year before, against West Virginia, he had caught two critical passes for touchdowns that propelled the Orange into a 15–12 win over the upset-minded Mountaineers and earned Syracuse a trip to the Orange Bowl.

DAVE BAKER (End): "I waited, oh how I waited, to be a part of this team of ours this fall. We're going to have one of the best damned teams there ever was. I really wanted to be a part of it. This has been a terrible year for me. I know all my buddies on the team will really do a job though. They will win every game they play. I only hope I get to play on a team this good next year."

Ben Schwartzwalder wasted no time in naming Gerhard Schwedes as his starting quarterback for the first game against Kansas. Although Dave Sarette was by far having the better of it in practices, Schwartzwalder still did not want to rush the talented youngster into the starting

Dave Baker. Courtesy of Syracuse University Sports Information.

lineup. It was one thing to do it in practices but quite another to do it in the games. Schwartzwalder was going to stick to his belief that until Sarette was able to prove himself in games he would remain on the second string. The old coach had great faith in Schwedes. He had proven himself as a player who could do well under pressure. This was only the first game of the year; there was a lot of football yet to be played. Schwartzwalder was going to bring young Sarette along slowly by not putting too much pressure on him early in the season. He knew Schwedes could handle the job. He was about to find out about Sarette.

Bob THOMAS

QUARTERBACK

I hurt my back in my freshman year during a punt return drill. I went to catch a short punt and was hit when my head was down. I kept having this pain in my right buttocks and a little bit down my leg. I thought it was a contusion. I played my sophomore and junior years, but it kept getting worse. Over the summer before my senior year I started experiencing some real pain. It got to the point where I was walking like Frankenstein, dragging a leg. We tried everything. We tried a chiropractor. Nothing helped.

"During the practices before the first game the pain kept getting worse. So they decided to send me down to an orthopedic doctor. He examined me. The doctor said, 'Bob, I know you want to play, but if you get hit wrong, you could be crippled for life.' So I went to the coach and told him what the doctor said. The Coach said, 'Well, you gotta do whatcha gotta do.' The unfortunate thing about this, Dave Baker was told that same day that he couldn't play either. I had to pack it in. Ben never spoke to me again. He never said a word.

"Two weeks before the Penn State game, I was told that Lee Andreas wanted to see me. He said, 'Look we got Sarette, and we're happy with him. We got Easterly, but we're a little dubious about Easterly. He can run hot and cold. Would you consider seeing another doctor? Get his opinion. Maybe you could suit up for Penn State. We won't use you unless we absolutely have to. Would you consider this?' I said sure. I went and saw another doctor, went through a series of tests. I'll never forget that they sent the results to the coaching staff, not to me. The results basically said I should not play football that year.

"A few weeks later, as my back continued to get worse, I went to see a doctor on my own. He said I should have an operation. I agreed. So over Thanksgiving I had it done. Well, someone told Ben that I had the back surgery. Lo and behold Ben shows up with his wife, with a care package of peanuts, cookies and such. He's talking to me, saying he hoped I would be able to come back next year. I did come back, but didn't play a hell of a lot. They already had Sarette and Easterly, both had a year of experience by then. Also, I had lost a couple of steps because of the operation. Unfortunately, I got hurt, but all in all, it was a good experience. That '59 team, I kind of wish back on what could have been."

Dave BAKER

END

I missed that frigging year. I'm still crying. Put that in your book! When I found out I couldn't play that year, I said, 'This is the best damned team there ever was, and it's going to be number one in the nation.' I knew I was not going to be able to play because the knee operations in those days took almost a whole year to heal. But I knew the guys were going to do it.

"I should have had an operation right after the Orange Bowl, but what happened is that they wrapped it up and I did exercises. My muscles, thigh muscles, never came back. Finally, the week before the season, I went down and it just crunched on me. They operated the next day, but I had no muscle in that leg and the rehabilitation went poorly. I may have to go to a knee replacement some day."

WILLIAM P. TOLLEY
Chancellor
Syracuse University

LEWIS P. ANDREAS
Director of Athletics
Syracuse University

Courtesy of Syracuse University Archives.

Gerhard Schwedes. Courtesy of Syracuse University Sports Information.

4

Captain

A knock at the door startled ten-year-old Gerhard Schwedes. The young boy got up from the table where he was finishing his schoolwork, turned down the radio, and moved toward the door. As Gerhard approached the door there was a second knock, strangely not as loud. Oddly, thoughts of his father raced through his mind. Could it be father? No, it couldn't be him, he thought. Father would not knock, he would come right in. As he slowly opened the door there stood his father, looking thin and jaundiced, a shadow of the man he remembered. Gerhard reached to put his arms around him.

"Don't touch me," the father said to his son. Gerhard Schwedes Sr. had been a soldier in the German army. He was a professional soldier, having enlisted in 1934. Captured in France in 1945, he had been held in a French prisoner of war camp these past three years. He had finally been released from prison. He was coming home dirty, lice-ridden, and very sickly. The ordeal of World War II was over for him at last. Today was his birthday. It was February 11, 1948. He was thirty-four years old.

The Great War, regardless of which side you were on, was difficult for all families around the world. In Germany, the Schwedes family was no exception. During the war each German family was given food rations. Gerhard's mother grew a garden and raised chickens to augment her family's meager daily allotment of food.

When Gerhard was four years old he saw Adolph Hitler. Hitler had spoken at a Regimental Exhibit near his home. Mothers lined their children up after his speech, and the children, one by one, would walk up and shake the Fueher's hand. Hitler rarely spoke.

The family had the radio on twenty four hours a day. The "Gundig Blaupunkt" broadcast the air raid warnings as soon as allied aircraft crossed over the German border. A 'Cookoo sound' would alert another incoming attack.

GERHARD SCHWEDES (Halfback): "As soon as a cookoo hit the radio you knew it was coming somewhere. If we had time we'd go into the country. If we didn't have time we would go into our bunkers. Every home, underneath, had doors three inches thick. They were pressure-proof. Sometimes they helped, sometimes they didn't. One evening when we were in the country we heard the cookoo. We found this cave, maybe a hundred yards deep. We talked to the families gathered there and they told us, 'Whenever we have time we come here, this is our protection. You are welcome here anytime.' Two weeks later a bomb directly hit that cave and killed them. There were about a hundred and eighty people in the cave at the time."

One morning in October, 1944, Gerhard's mother called to him to come to the front door of their house. An open hearse containing the body of German Field Marshall Erwin Rommel, 'The Desert Fox' was passing their front door.

Rommel, born in Heidenheim an der Brentz near Ulm in 1891, realized that Germany could not possibly win the war. He no longer supported Hitler in its continuance. Injured in a strafing air attack, he was recovering from injuries in a French hospital. Although not personally involved with Hitler's overthrow, he was later implicated. Assigned to house arrest in the French hospital, he was given the choice of committing suicide or being killed as a traitor. Fearing for his family's safety, Rommel took his own life on October 14, 1944 at a hospital in Ulm. Hitler attempted in vain to keep Rommel's death from the German people. The people wanted to see their greatest general. Thousands had turned out to pay their respects. Gerhard's family, like the rest of the German families, only knew what the Nazi propaganda machine had told them.

GERHARD SCHWEDES (Halfback): "The German people were very misinformed. I don't think they heard everything. No excuses. It was tough. It was really hard."

The population of Gerhard's village was sixty thousand. In one night alone planes came and killed five thousand. Throughout the first eight years of his life Gerhard went to bed every night clutching a blanket in his hand with a gas mask laid on top of it.

GERHARD SCHWEDES (Halfback): "That's the way it was. That is the way I was brought up. We did not think anything any different. I mean, didn't everybody in the rest of the world live like that?"

Gerhard's favorite game was playing "Cowboys and Indians" with his friends.

GERHARD SCHWEDES (Halfback): "We had the feathers, we had the cowboy hats, we would play in the fields. More than a half dozen times the planes would come after us . . . 'rat-ta-tat-tat, rat-ta-tat-tat' . . . their guns shooting at us. It was unreal."

Once Hitler's Third Reich was defeated the rations stopped. Because there was no money and no rations the family bartered for everything. Germany was now under Allied forces occupation. There were twenty thousand American soldiers located in the Town of Ulm where Gerhard lived. Gerhard's mother and grandmother would do the soldiers' laundry. In exchange, the soldiers would give them a brick of soap. His mother would carefully slice the soap and trade ninety percent of it for meat, clothing, vegetables, or anything the family needed. Tobacco was a big bartering item. Every night Gerhard would walk the streets collecting discarded cigarette butts from the GIs. He would slice off the burnt ends and load a cigar box with the unused tobacco. The tobacco was like gold to Gerhard and his family. He would barter a box of his loose tobacco for three chickens, a bunch of rabbits, shoes, or anything else they needed to survive. At night the Army would set up chow lines to feed the soldiers. The American GIs loved kids. Each evening Gerhard would get four empty tomato cans with hooks attached so he could hold them. The GIs would take him through their chow line and fill the cans with food. Whatever the GIs had that night for dinner the Schwedes family had the same.

Occupied Germany at that time was under a curfew. Every night at nine o'clock sharp the citizens of Ulm, upon hearing the fire whistle blow, were required to immediately go to their homes. Anyone found out after curfew was arrested. Once the German people were in their homes, the GIs would go out into the deserted streets and play football or softball under the lights. The young German children, envious, watched the American soldiers play from their windows. If any ball mistakenly was left outside, the German kids grabbed it.

GERHARD SCHWEDES (Halfback): "We used the softballs to play soccer and we had no idea what the hell to do with the footballs. We called the football 'eierball,' which in German meant egg ball. We would sell the footballs back to the GIs the next day for a can of food or whatever else we might need. The American soldiers were absolutely terrific. They were dynamite and took really good care of us kids."

Life in war-ravaged Germany after the war was difficult. The Schwedes family did what they could to survive. Gerhard's father eventually regained his strength and found work as a policeman on the German railroad.

During the occupation the German kids had formed a close bond with the American GIs. The soldiers had regaled the young German boys with stories about America which they in turn would share with their families at night. As a result, all the members of the Schwedes family longed to go to America. Each yearned for a chance to have a better life.

Gerhard's uncle on his father's side had immigrated to the United States twenty-one years before. He had settled in New Jersey where he learned the butcher trade. Eventually he was able to own his own butcher shop and became quite successful. Letters back and forth between the relatives finally culminated in a plan for the Schwedes family to immigrate to the United States. It had been arranged for young Gerhard's father to be contracted to go to work for his brother.

On December 15, 1949, the Schwedes family boarded a ship and set sail for the United States.

GERHARD SCHWEDES (Halfback): "We came over just before Christmas in 1949. The most impressive thing I have ever seen in my whole life, really, was the neon lights. I had never seen a neon light in my life. My aunt took me to a restaurant and a grocery store that had neon lights. It flabbergasted me. I had never ever seen anything like that before in my whole life."

When the family landed in the United States, they went to live with an aunt in Irvington, New Jersey. The uncle's butcher shop was located forty miles away in the rural town of Clinton and Gerhard's father had to make the long trip each day to work for his brother. Unfortunately, life as a butcher didn't last long for him. The two brothers argued constantly. Gerhard's father felt his brother was overbearing and finally, in a fit of rage, quit. He walked out and never spoke to his brother again.

Rough financial times returned to the Schwedes family. Work for his father was sparse. He finally, through the efforts of the Whitehead family who lived next door, found a job. Gifted with skillful hands, he found employment as a handyman with a company near their home. Gerhard's mother, equally as talented as her husband, took a job as a scamstress.

GERHARD SCHWEDES (Halfback): "My mother found a job as a seamstress. As far-fetched as you may think this is, she hitchhiked to work every morning, fifteen miles to her job. My dad had to be to work at seven, she had to be to work at nine, so there was a time conflict. It was a rural area and she hitchhiked every day to work. We needed the money and she had no other way of getting there so she hitchhiked every day."

Speaking English wasn't a problem for Gerhard in his new country. German schools had required students to learn two foreign languages, French and English. He had an aptitude for language and learned quickly. The American GIs had been a big help to him in understanding English. Learning new sports, on the other hand, was a bigger challenge to this ultra-competitive youngster. In Germany he had played soccer, competed on the junior field hockey team, and had been a top swimmer on the local swim team. Most German families encouraged their children to be active in athletics. Gerhard and his two older brothers were constantly playing some sport when their family chores were done.

GERHARD SCHWEDES (Halfback): "When I came over to this country I was eleven and a half. I tried playing these strange sports. Basketball came naturally. Baseball was hard and football was really an enigma. I went out for the freshman team in high school and had no clue what the hell the sport was about. In fact, my father wouldn't let me play. My closest friend, Norman Yetman, was a minister's son, and my parents and his parents were close. The minister wouldn't let his son play football either. He went to his father and said, 'Gerhard's parents are letting him play,' and I went to my parents and said, 'Norman's parents are letting him play,' and we both were allowed to play football. They made me a punter because I could kick. But no one taught me that the ball is supposed to be held long wise to produce the spiral. I held the ball straight across and kicked it as hard as I could. Unfortunately nobody knew where it was going and neither did I. I finally ended up starting as a freshman on the varsity team at halfback. That first year I played on the worst team that my high school had ever had. The last game we played Washington. They were 0–8, and we were 0–8. They beat 'the living bejesus out of us,' so we were 0–9.

"My high school career in sports was tough. We had only four hundred students in the entire school. It was tough to compete with the bigger schools. We had a great basketball team but a lousy football team."

In high school Gerhard played football, basketball and baseball. A natural athlete, he excelled in football and basketball. Following his junior year he received a letter from the University of Maryland football office expressing their interest in him. Gerhard also received a few other letters regarding football from smaller schools and a possible basketball scholarship to Bradley University. Gerhard wanted to play major college football. He visited Maryland during his senior year. He liked the football coaches, the players, and the history of the school. In his mind that's where he was going. Maryland had been showing interest in him right along so he was sure they were going to offer him a scholarship. It never happened. Gerhard waited too long for Maryland to make a decision. By that late date the other schools interested in him had already signed other players.

GERHARD SCHWEDES (Halfback): "Fortunately, my high school football coach had been in the Navy with Rocco Pirro, the Syracuse line coach. Talk about serendipity. He called Rocco and said, 'I have a kid that could really help you.' I got the last scholarship that Syracuse had to offer that year. If it wasn't for my high school football coach knowing Rocco Pirro I may have ended up playing some bad basketball at Bradley.

"When I got to Syracuse they put me at fullback (on the freshmen team) and moved me behind two high school All-Americans, Steve Novak and Jim Anderson. Both were highly sought after high school players. So we start the first game and I was the third string fullback. Halfway through the game, I knew I would play a lot of football. By the time the game had ended, I KNEW I was going to start the next game. And I did! I went to Syracuse with an attitude that I had something to prove and that's the way I was throughout my entire college career."

Bill BELL

ASSISTANT COACH

Gerhard Schwedes was an over-achiever. He wasn't blessed with natural talent and he worked for everything he got. He was very smart, and on the football field, he knew how to get things done. He was a real leader who played with a lot of confidence."

Maury YOUMANS
TACKLE

Gerhard gave 100 percent, in every minute of every ball game. He might be dead tired, and he may have ran out for two or three passes in a row, but he would always come back to the huddle, full of fire. He would keep everyone going. He was our leader."

Ken Erickson scores six against Kansas. Courtesy of Syracuse
University Archives.

Kansas

Ben Schwartzwalder watched his team intently as they completed their last workout in preparation for their opening game against Kansas. The past three weeks of practice had been grueling. He had driven his team hard, challenging each player physically and mentally, asking them to give more when they had no more to give. The coach had been uncompromising. He expected a level of performance that in the players minds was unrealistic. They had practiced for hours under unforgiving heat that had sapped their strength. He demanded they push on. His coaching staff verbally abused them for every mistake. Praise was rare and the challenge of the competition within the team was great. Schwartzwalder knew this group was special. They had taken everything he had thrown at them and came back for more. This was his way of finding out if they could handle the pressure. Nine months of rehashing the Oklahoma loss ate at his insides.

Football was Ben Schwartzwalder's life. He worked hard and he knew he was a good coach. This year's team was strong. It had a nice blend of talented young players and seasoned lettermen. The lack of experience at quarterback was a concern but he had confidence that Schwedes and Sarette would come through when it counted. Schwartzwalder felt his quarterbacks had to play well for his team to beat Kansas. He was confident that Kansas couldn't stop his team's running game. He wondered if any team could. On the other hand, his starting defensive front line had yet to play up to its capabilities. In fact, the second group had out-preformed the first team on defense the past three weeks. He hoped the defensive changes his coaches had made during the past week would help.

JOE SZOMBATHY (Assistant Coach): "Before the Kansas game, in our last scrimmage, we were just so upset that the first team looked so bad on defense. We couldn't imagine what the hell was wrong. Guys were running through us like water through a sieve. We were pretty well set on what guys should play where and we really didn't want to make any changes. We felt going into preseason practices that the first team would be solid on defense. But to be honest, we did not look good at all.

"We were (the whole defensive staff) walking off the field, shaking our heads, and Ben says, 'Jesus, I don't know what happened today but that defense looked bad.' We decided . . . let's regroup. We decided we looked too predictable. We would now have our defensive line begin jumping at the line of scrimmage into different defensive formations. Sometimes we would start with the tackles wide in a five-three, then shift to a regular six-tight, or we may start in a six-man line and shift to an eight-man line depending upon the situation. We began practicing that and we started looking better each day prior to the Kansas game. Ben was really pleased with the improvement. We all were."

The first game each year was always the hardest for the old coach. He had prepared his team as best he could, but until they played that first game, he was never sure what he had. He just hoped he had selected the right people to play. Schwartzwalder was concerned about the health of the Syracuse kicking game. Both Tom Gilburg, his punter, and Bob Yates, his place kicker, were banged up going into the game. He hoped they would be able to perform. There were so many things to worry about.

Schwartzwalder, blowing his whistle, called his team together. "Boys," he said, staring down at the ground, "Tomorrow will be our opportunity to show people what kind of football team we are. Make no mistake: This Kansas bunch will be ready to play. They should have beaten TCU last week and they're gunning to upset us." Schwartz-walder, his voice rising slightly, added, "We are NOT going to let that happen!" Turning his eyes toward his captain, Gerhard Schwedes, he said, "I have complete confidence that this team will win this battle to-morrow. We have worked hard. Everyone has paid the price. It's time to go to war. Everyone here accept this challenge and let's go kick the hell out of Kansas for sixty minutes." The players cheered.

The Kansas Jawhawkers (later to be shortened to the Jayhawks), were coached by former Oklahoma quarterback, Jackie Mitchell. Mitchell, who had been an All-American at Oklahoma, brought a young but talented team to Archbold Stadium. Eleven of the top twenty-two players were sophomores. Against Syracuse, Kansas would start two of these youngsters in its backfield. John Hadl and Curtis Mc-Clinton. Hadl (who later went onto a great career in the NFL as a quarterback for the San Diego Chargers) lined up at left halfback. Mc-Clinton, who would also play professionally, was the fullback. The Jay-hawkers lost their opening game of the season the Saturday before to nationally ranked TCU, 14–7. Jackie Mitchell's young team had played TCU even for three quarters before losing the game on a punt return late in the contest.

The young Kansas coach's ties to Oklahoma had the Syracuse coaching staff concerned. They hoped Kansas wouldn't have the Okla-homa blueprint on how to shut down the Syracuse ground game. The Sooners had stopped the Orange's running game cold in the Orange Bowl. Oklahoma, at times using an eight-man-line, had smothered Syracuse's backs along the line of scrimmage. The staff was worried that Kansas would do the same.

Saturday, September 26, 1959, was a beautiful fall day for a foot-ball game with clear blue skies and temperatures in the mid-seventies. Syracuse took the opening kickoff before 25,000 fans and steadily marched down the field behind the strong running of fullback Art Baker. Reaching the Kansas 32-yard line, Syracuse was faced with a fourth and one. Ben Schwartzwalder had his first big decision to make. Should he try for the field goal and put 3 points on the board, or go for the first down? Syracuse kicker Bob Yates easily had the range to kick a 42-yard field goal. Schwartzwalder decided to go for it. Ernie Davis, running off-tackle, was stopped inches short of the first down. Kansas took over on downs.

The Jawhawkers' first three running plays netted four yards and they were forced to punt. The teams continued to trade possessions with no points being scored the rest of the first quarter. Syracuse had continued to move the ball, racking up first downs, but each drive had stalled because of mistakes and penalties.

Early in the second period, while facing a third and seven, Kansas's John Hadl 'quick-kicked.' The ball hit on the Syracuse 21 and rolled dead on the 15-yard line. The punt had traveled 59 yards. Syracuse was penalized on the play for clipping which now pushed the ball back to the Orangemen's 2-yard line. Syracuse, backed up to their own goal line, gained eight yards on three running plays setting up a critical punting situation. Schwartzwalder's first thought was to get one of his two more experienced centers, Dave Applehof or Al Bemiller, into the game to make this important snap. He gambled and left sophomore center Bob Stem in the game. Schwartzwalder, with the new wildcard substitution rule, was allowed to change one player, but he decided against it. Stem's snap to punter Tom Gilburg was short, bouncing two yards in front of the startled punter. Gilburg picked up the ball and realized it would be impossible for him to punt. Dodging one tackler in the end zone, Gilburg saw an open space up the right side of the field. Running as hard as he could he broke one tackle before two Kansas players hit him at the same time, knocking him down at the Syracuse 6-yard line. Kansas had the first big break of the game.

The Jayhawkers, on three straight running plays, moved the ball to the Syracuse 1-yard line as the first period came to a close. Coach Jackie Mitchell knew that trying to get one yard against the big Syracuse line would be tough. Mitchell decided to try an option pass. Kansas quarterback, Duane Morris, faking a handoff to the fullback, pitched the ball to halfback John Hadl who sprinted to the outside. Hadl looked toward the end zone and spotted Curtis McClinton wide open. The young sophomore hurriedly threw the pass on the run, overthrowing the open receiver. Syracuse had held on fourth down but one of the Syracuse players had lined up offside giving Kansas another chance. With the ball six inches from the goal line, Mitchell decided to run it.

Quarterback Duane Morris took the snap, stayed low, and dove over the goal line for the game's first score. The Kansas extra point was good. The visitors had a 7–0 lead.

High in the press box above Archbold stadium, Assistant Coach Roy Simmons noticed something about the Kansas defense. As the game went on the Jawhawkers defensive backs began moving closer and closer to the line of scrimmage. Simmons knew it was time to throw the ball. It was time to put Syracuse's best passer in the game. It was time to take a look at Dave Sarette. Simmons called down to Schwartzwalder and said, "Pappy, we need to throw the ball. Let's give Sarette a chance." Schwartzwalder at that moment was disgusted with his team's mistakes. They were pushing Kansas all over the field, leading in statistics, but trailing in points. Ben finally listened to his longtime aide and put Sarette in the game.

DAVE SARETTE (Quarterback): "Roy Simmons was one of my backers all the way. So in the game against Kansas we were losing to them. We had been moving the ball but we needed to throw. Roy Simmons, who was up in the press box, called down to Schwartzwalder and said, 'Send Sarette in . . . Send Sarette in and let him throw a pass.' Schwartzwalder comes over and grabs me and says, 'Okay, go in and throw the boom opposite pass.' I said okay and I ran in. This was my first game and my knees were kind of weak. I go in and I made the fake on the boom opposite pass and I set up (to pass). I look downfield and there's a man deep and he's wide open. Also there's a man under him and he's wide open. They were just both wide open. I didn't know who to throw to and ended up letting it go in between, missing both of them. I look over to the sidelines and I see Schwartzwalder, hands in the air, going over and grabbing Schwedes.

"I knew I had one chance in life. I huddled them up as quick as I could and I said, 'Same play on one.' Schwedes was part way out and I sent him back. I waved him off the field. I got under the center, same exact play, and Erickson was wide open in the end zone. I hit him for a touchdown. That saved my life. I started with the first team the rest of the time."

Schwartzwalder was so excited over the touchdown that he decided to go for two points on the conversion with another pass. This time Kansas was ready and Sarette's pass to Erickson was intercepted in the end zone. Despite the fact that Syracuse was behind 7–6, Ben Schwartzwalder felt he'd had found himself a quarterback.

There was no more scoring as the teams headed for the dressing room at halftime. Kansas led where it counted most. The scoreboard read 7–6 thanks in part to the tremendous quick-kicking by John Hadl. The Kansas sophomore had pinned Syracuse back twice with quick-kicks. The second one traveled an amazing 72 yards. Although Syracuse was dominating the game and the statistics, Kansas still had the lead.

Curtis McClinton took Bob Yates's second half kickoff at the 6-yard line and returned it to his own 27. On the first play from scrimmage, Hadl running wide, gained three yards before he was hit hard by Roger Davis and fumbled. Schwedes, coming up from his defensive back position, dove on the loose pigskin and recovered the ball on the Kansas 37-yard line.

Sticking to his game plan, Schwartzwalder had Schwedes start the second half at quarterback. Schwedes, rolling left off the option, faked a pitch out to Ernie Davis and rambled 17 yards for a Syracuse first down at the Kansas 20-yard line. Junior halfback Whitey Reimer, all of 158 pounds, was inserted into the lineup replacing an injured Mark Weber. Reimer's first carry gained 11 yards off-tackle, giving Syracuse a first down just inside the Kansas 10-yard line. After two straight running plays netted two yards, Schwedes rolled right and threw the ball to left end Jerry Skonieczki. He made a leaping catch between two Kansas defenders for Syracuse's second score. With his team now leading 12–7, Schwartzwalder decided to go for two again. Schwedes attempted a pass to Reimer over the middle but it was overthrown.

Bob Yates' short line drive kickoff was taken by John Hadl at the 9-yard line. Without breaking stride the speedy Hadl ran straight up the middle finding a huge hole in the Syracuse defense and galloped 91-yards untouched for a touchdown.

Syracuse's first lead in the game had lasted twelve seconds.

With Kansas again in the lead, 13–12, Jackie Mitchell decided to go for two. The Kansas coach called for a halfback option, the same play that had failed earlier. This time Hadl hit McClinton with a perfect

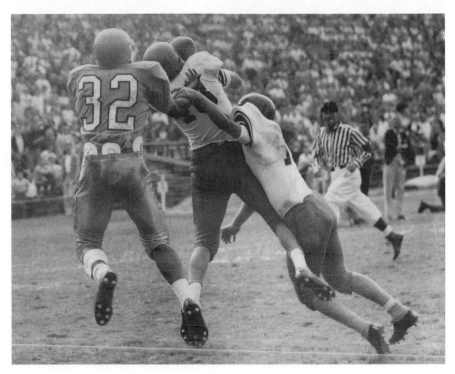
Ed Bowers intercepts against Kansas. Courtesy of Gerhard Schwedes.

pass for the two-point conversion. Kansas now led the favored Orangemen 15–12.

Schwartzwalder decided to switch to Sarette at quarterback. Behind the power running of Jim Anderson, Syracuse steadily moved the ball down the field to a first down at the Kansas 14-yard line. On the ensuing play, Anderson ran to his left, took a pitch from Sarette, and blasted his way down to the Jayhawkers 2. Three straight running plays netted no yards. Facing another fourth down decision, Schwartzwalder again passed up a sure three points. He called a quarterback option off the ride series. Sarette took the snap and slid down the line of scrimmage looking for an opening. Just as Kansas tackle John Peppercorn reached to grab Sarette's arm, the alert quarterback tossed the ball to reserve fullback John Nichols who dove into the end zone for the touchdown. Syracuse was back in the lead 18–15.

Schwartzwalder decided for two again. Sarette, taking the snap from center Dave Applehof, moved left to hand off to Jim Anderson who was cutting back toward the right side. The young quarterback slipped the ball between the powerful running back's arms. Anderson, poised to take the ball, was looking straight ahead, searching for a place to run. Up front, the powerful Syracuse line, unbalanced to the right, moved forward. Left guard Roger Davis had pulled out and run to his right appearing to lead Anderson into the end zone. Seeing this, the Kansas defense instinctively moved right in anticipation of Syracuse's power sweep. At the last possible second Sarette pulled the ball away from Anderson. He placed the ball on his left hip and sprinted left towards the end zone. The Kansas players were totally fooled and tried to recover but it was too late. Sarette crossed the goal line without a Kansas defender within 10 yards of him. Syracuse led 20–15.

In the fourth quarter Syracuse marched down the field again behind the running of Art Baker. Baker would carry six times in the drive which included a powerful 20-yard run through the middle of the undermanned Kansas defense. Syracuse went 64 yards for the score with Schwedes (now operating at halfback) getting the touchdown from two yards out. Syracuse again went for two. Sarette found Skonieczki over the middle to push the lead to 28–15.

Kansas tried to rally on the next series but Hadl, on a roll-out, was hit hard by Maury Youmans and fumbled. The Orange recovered at the 27-yard line. A personal foul against the now frustrated Jayhawkers moved the ball to the Kansas 12-yard line. Schwedes scored three plays later. Yates' extra point gave the Orangemen a 35–15 lead.

Late in the final period, with Syracuse reserves in the game, they misplayed a punt, giving Kansas the ball at the Orange's 26-yard line. The Kansas offense moved the ball to the Syracuse 13 where Hadl scampered up the middle for the game's last touchdown. The final score was 35–21.

Syracuse out gained Kansas 493 yards to 67. Sarette, in his first varsity contest, was 9–13 passing. He threw for 117 yards and one touchdown. Schwedes, in his quarterback debut, hit on 5 of 6 passes for 40 yards and one score. The Syracuse ground game that punished Kansas all day was led by Art Baker. He carried the ball 18 times for 92 yards. Ernie Davis, also in his first varsity game, garnered just 30 yards on 10 carries.

Kansas sophomore back John Hadl had clearly outplayed his Syracuse counterpart. Besides scoring two touchdowns, Hadl completed one pass for a 2-point conversion and averaged 69 yards on two quick-kicks. Many of the veteran press that day thought Hadl was the most talented halfback any visiting team had brought to Archbold Stadium in years.

JACKIE MITCHELL (Kansas Head Coach): "Syracuse was the best offensive team we've played in a long, long time. I never believed any team would score 35 points in a game against us but they sure earned them all. We tried to stunt our defenses (similar to Oklahoma in the Orange Bowl) to make up for their power. We just couldn't handle them. Syracuse is a very good football team."

JOE SZOMBATHY (Assistant Coach): "We had designated one player on defense to make the call which told the linemen when to shift. A new rule had come out stating that you can't use a double-syllable word and the referee was telling us in the Kansas game we couldn't use that word anymore. 'Red dog.' Ted Dailey said, 'Well we got to come up with another word.' He looked at Bruce Tarbox and said, 'Bruce, what's your girlfriend's name?' Bruce says, 'Sally.' Ted says, 'Alright then, that's going to be our word. Every time we were ready to jump defenses, yell Sally.' The rest of the year, we would yell, 'Sally,' then everybody would shift."

MAURY YOUMANS (Tackle): "I thought at halftime we were going to get beat. They were a better team that first half. They came into town with more of a reputation than we had. We were still the Eastern team, and they supposedly played a better brand of football. I'm sure there was a psychological aspect that this was maybe a better team than us. I think we came out that second half and really found ourselves. I think we began to come together. It was early in the season which was very fortunate for us. A lot of the sophomores began to show just how good they were."

Schwartzwalder was relieved to get this game over. His team had totally dominated the contest. Kansas had scored all three touchdowns on Syracuse mistakes. The Orange had truly owned the line of scrimmage. After the game the veteran coach told his team, "We got by this one okay, boys. Now let's get down to business and get ready for Maryland."

Arnie BURDICK

SPORTS EDITOR, *HERALD JOURNAL,* 1959

The schedule was different from the usual Northeastern slate that Orange footballers were called upon to play. A Big Eight team (Kansas) was the opener, and a Pacific Coast team (UCLA) was the closer, with a pair of teams from Maryland (Navy and Maryland) in the middle. It was the first time Syracuse had ever played Kansas, Navy and UCLA in football. It was also the first time Syracuse played a football game on the West Coast since 1924, 35 years ago. There was more than just happenstance that this "Nationwide" schedule, came together for the '59 Orangemen.

"In the early 1950s, soon after World War II, there was considerable talk in collegiate athletic circles about forming a "National Airplane Conference" that would embrace such independents as Syracuse, Pitt, Penn State, Army, Navy as well as UCLA, USC on the West Coast, Kansas, and Nebraska from the Mid-west.

"Some of the movers and shakers were the athletic directors, Lew Andreas (Syracuse), Tom Hamilton(Pitt), Ernie McCoy(Penn State), Dutch Lonborg(Kansas), and Wilbur Johns (UCLA).

"It so happens that Andreas, Lonborg and Johns were all long time basketball coaches who had retired from active court duty to the AD chair. Hamilton was one of the more influential athletic directors in the game, a former AD at Navy who was moving through Pitt on his way to soon becoming commissioner of the Pacific Coast Conference.

"In retrospect, it's probably a godsend that this type of a national slate confronted the '59 team, rather than the usual Northeastern schedule. For when the season-ending polls were being voted on, the far ranging, national scope of the slate was a huge factor in weighing support for Syracuse."

Roy Simmons. Courtesy of Syracuse University Archives.

Recruiting the Team

"We were the luckiest guys in the world. We just happened to get a bunch of kids to gel. Easterly, Youmans, Tarbox, Schwedes, nobody wanted any of these kids. Why, when Bob Yates was a sophomore, we were wishing he'd quit. He grew up, but he was rinky dink until he was a junior. We have the same kids we've been getting right along. Actually we missed most of the kids we were really after, and had to settle for the kids we took."
 —Roy Simmons,
  Assistant Coach

The "Syracuse Society of Bird Dogs," is how Ben Schwartzwalder described them. This group of loyal fans would provide tips to coaches on outstanding athletes in their respective areas. These 'bird dogs' would also talk to potential recruits about the benefits of going to Syracuse. Once Syracuse settled on a recruit, a questionnaire would be sent out to the player, his coach, his principal, and his parents. A form was included that asked permission to talk with the recruit, provided he had an interest in going to Syracuse. A master list was built from this information and coaches were then dispatched to their assigned areas. Once a lad was chosen Schwartzwalder's next move was to talk with his principal. With a limited number of scholarships available, the old coach wanted to make sure he could get the new recruit into school, and more importantly, keep him eligible for football. Evaluation of the recruits was very important.

BEN SCHWARTZWALDER: "If a kid has an IQ of 130 and a 'C' average, I don't want him, he's lazy. If he plays football, he'll loaf. Another thing . . . you ask a kid how much football means to him and he says, 'I can take it or leave it,' I don't want him. Of course, if he was really good, then everyone wants him and we don't get him. Each year we lose four or five boys who we felt would have been our first string frosh fullback . . . We lose 'em to Notre Dame, BC, Army, Navy and the Ivies all the time."

The "Rodney Dangerfield" of head football coaches in the fifties felt he got more respect and results recruiting athletes from smaller schools.

BEN SCHWARTZWALDER: "We look for bigger boys in smaller schools."

BILL BELL (Assistant Coach): "We always felt that the number one thing that you had to have first was an athlete. Second, he had to have an attitude. If you had an athlete and he didn't have an attitude then you really didn't have anybody. You had to have someone that you could depend on each day. We always looked first for the athlete but he had to be able to run and always he had to be strong. Of course you get some of these little skinny kids that prove you wrong but that's what we looked for."

JERRY SKONIECZKI (End): "I tell people all the time that Ben Schwartzwalder loved to recruit ends because they were agile. Also, he liked it if they were basketball players. He loved that combination. Next, he would want fullbacks, because fullbacks always got contact. If they didn't make it at fullback at Syracuse many of them would be transformed into linebackers. Our '59 team, many of the guys who played inside, were ends in high school. Maury Youmans, Roger Davis and Al Bemiller were all ends in high school. Each one of those guys also played basketball. Bruce Tarbox, who played guard, was actually a halfback in high school. Bob Yates was the only one of us who played tackle in high school, but he did play basketball. Fred Mautino and myself, who were the ends in '59 on the first team, were both ends and basketball players in high school."

The "bird dogs" had much to do with the makeup of the '59 team. Many of the players that contributed to the team's success, were the results of the alumni's help. Art Baker, the outstanding fullback from Erie, Pennsylvania, was recruited by a Syracuse alumni who ran the local radio station there. Baker, an outstanding wrestler, went to Syracuse because he could wrestle and play football. Baker, who had aspirations of being a professional football player, felt going to Syracuse gave him the best of both worlds. As it turned out, he was right. Baker won the NCAA 191-pound crown as a sophomore and went on to a professional football career in Canada.

MAURY YOUMANS (Tackle): "I didn't plan on going to college originally until sports intervened. I had another half year of high school left and I needed some college credits. I went to Dean Academy in Worcester, Massachusetts and got my grades up. I also took, and passed, the courses I needed to qualify for college. I had another pretty good year in football and basketball at Dean.

"Roy Simmons' wife was probably the biggest reason for my going to Syracuse. My father did some part-time work for them and kept them abreast of my progress. I was planning to go to Bucknell. Mrs. Simmons went to Ben Schwartzwalder and said, 'You need to have that Youmans boy. You give that Youmans boy a scholarship.' I heard she cornered him one day at a party and convinced him to offer me a scholarship. That was all I needed. I knew I was going to be close to home so I accepted the scholarship. Schwartzwalder talked with the Syracuse basketball coach, Mark Guley, about the offer possibly being a basketball scholarship. Guley was interested in me but they only had five scholarships available. Football had fifteen scholarships so they gave me a football scholarship. Ben told me I could play both. He indicated I could quit football after the first year if it didn't work out. So I really had no plans to play football past the first year."

FRED MAUTINO (End): "My brother Lou and I had decided that we wanted to go to the same college and play football together. Penn State was recruiting me hard but did not want to offer Lou a scholarship. I told them that if they didn't take my brother than I wasn't going to go there. They said, 'no.' They were not offering Lou a scholarship. Syracuse, on the other hand said they would take Lou and that's how I ended up at Syracuse. It was a great experience to go there."

ROGER DAVIS (Guard): "There was a guy from my hometown in Ohio that was a Syracuse University graduate. He was a big recruiter for Syracuse. He lived in the Briar Hill area in Solon. I think his name was Lowe. He spoke to me first about Syracuse. I went up there and I liked it better by far of anywhere I went. I went down and looked at Alabama and then visited Bowling Green. That was the only two schools I looked at. Most of the letters I received from other schools I did not bother responding to. I knew I was going to go to Syracuse because of this guy Lowe and because I liked it when I went up there. I thought the atmosphere was good. At Alabama you didn't even live with the other students. Football had its own dorm. You know it was more like a job. I didn't care for it. Also, I liked Ben right off. Bill Bell was there too. I thought Ben was a great coach because of the way he would change things. We weren't 'three yards and a cloud of dust,' like a lot of teams were back then. A good example of what I'm saying was starting off the Cotton Bowl with that long pass. Also, he was the boss. A lot of the coaches today aren't anymore. Especially when they have a bad team. He ran the show. The troops weren't in charge of the asylum as it is with a lot of teams. A perfect example of what I am talking about was when I went from the Chicago Bears to the Los Angeles Rams. I couldn't believe the Rams. It soured me on pro football. At that time the Rams had way better personnel than the Bears and we had won the championship in 1963. These guys couldn't even play five hundred ball. Just look at the defensive line they had . . . Deacon Jones, Rosie Grier, Merlin Olsen . . . I mean what the hell more do you need? We played the Bears the first year I was with the Rams and the Bears killed us. I couldn't believe it."

DAVE SARETTE (Quarterback): "The first time I had ever heard of Syracuse was in 1957 when Jim Brown was playing in the Cotton Bowl. There was a gentleman by the name of Driscoll. He had gone to Syracuse. He had opened up a business in Dover, New Hampshire. He loved Syracuse football. Evidently he had heard about me. He came to some of my games, watched me play, and then recommended me to Syracuse. At the time, I was being recruited by quite a few schools.

"After Syracuse saw films of me playing, they started recruiting me to go to school there. I can remember going up with Driscoll for a visit to Syracuse. I remember going on the New York State Thruway. Now you're talking to a guy who at that time had never been further than fifty miles from his home. I can remember the rhythmic beat of the car going over the concrete lines. Ba-bomb, ba-bomb. Anyway, getting to Syracuse was great. I mean, it was a big school and to me it would be the one place that I would like to go to. I wanted to play good football and I made the right decision to go there."

JERRY SKONIECZKI (End): "My high school football coach was a great athlete who had boxed for Roy Simmons at Syracuse. His name was Francis "Moon" Mullins. He was also a friend of Ben's. He told the coaching staff about me and I was invited up for a visit. While I was there they offered me a scholarship and I accepted. Colgate, Delaware and Colby had shown interest in me. I never contemplated going to any of those schools. I remember at the time I was being re-cruited seeing a picture in the paper of Jim Brown scoring a touch-down against Army. That did it for me. I just wanted to play in old Archbold Stadium.

"I remember the first time I met Ben. I of course had heard about him being an ex-paratrooper and how tough he was. Anyway, he looked at me over his glasses and he says, "Well, Skonieczki, you're 181 pounds now. By your senior year we'll have you at 220.' I don't know how the hell he knew that but in my senior year I was playing at 220 pounds."

JOHN BROWN (Tackle): "One of the referees for my high school games played for Ben at Muhlenberg. He was refereeing one of my games and asked afterwards if had I heard of Syracuse. He went on to tell me he had played for the coach of Syracuse and that he was going to call him and mention me to him. That's what he did and Ben called and asked if we had any game films. We did and my coach sent the game film up to Ben. Ben then called back and asked me to come up and visit and I did. Jim Brown showed me around and of course that was very impressive. I decided to matriculate at Syracuse. I was looking at The University of Pennsylvania and Rutgers. Also, I had heard from all the black schools down south . . . Florida A&M, Maryland State, Morgan State . . . all of those.

"Jim Brown was very influential in getting me to Syracuse. He took me around, told me about Syracuse and the opportunities there. Of course everything had been going well for him. He thought it was a school that was just now getting used to.the black athlete. He felt it would be a good experience for me."

AL BEMILLER (Center): "I got to Syracuse through my wrestling. I was the national prep school heavyweight wrestling champion in Pennsylvania. The coach at Syracuse wanted me for wrestling but they did not have any scholarships left. He went to Schwartzwalder and told him I also played football. That's how I got my scholarship. I wasn't supposed to go there. I didn't have any thoughts of going to Syracuse. I didn't even know where Syracuse was. When I won the championship it was my coach that wanted me to go to Syracuse so that's why I went. I originally was going to go to Gettysburg College on a scholarship. My marks weren't good enough so I ended up going to prep school. I paid my own tuition at prep school, so I was not obligated to anyone."

BOB YATES (Tackle): "My high school coach was a graduate of Syracuse.He was in the class of 1948. He steered me that way. Originally my first choice was Army. I wanted to go to West Point but I didn't have the grades to get in so my second choice was Syracuse. It was an easy pick.

"When I left high school I was a big kid, probably the biggest kid in the state of Vermont. I got down there and I felt like a midget. I felt kind of like a small fish in a big pond."

TOM GILBURG (End): "I was working at a day camp down in White Plains, New York and I was actually planning to go to the University of South Carolina. The director of the camp was a Syracuse grad and his brother was a banker up in Syracuse. One day he calls me over the loudspeaker to come to the office. I go in the office and Ben's there. Ben started talking to me about Syracuse and I said, 'I'm sorry coach, but I'm all set. I'm going to South Carolina.' I told him I was committed to go to South Carolina. So that was it, I thought. Two weeks later I get another call over the loudspeaker to come up to the office. I go up to the office and the director says, 'Tom, you go home. Your high school coach has some people he wants you to talk to.' So I go home and Ben is there with John Hafner, the Director of Admissions at Syracuse. I sat down with Ben and I just couldn't say no. I said, 'Alright I'm coming to Syracuse.' So I had to send all the stuff back to South Carolina and that's how I ended up in Syracuse. I guess that's one of the reasons they have all these recruiting rules now."

DAVE BAKER (End): "I went to prep school and this guy came to my house. I had no idea who he was. He was some kind of scout from around New England for Syracuse and he talked to me and he said, 'Are you interested in Syracuse?' I told him I would love to go there. My father had gone there. He had crewed for Syracuse which was big in those days. This scout said he would make arrangements for me to visit. So I got on a plane a couple of weeks later and went to see the campus. Les Dye (Freshman coach) met me. He took me around the campus. I loved it! I got an offer for a full scholarship and I took it."

MARK WEBER (Halfback): "Roger Davis and I played on the same high school team. He was a year ahead of me. My senior year I got a 1957 Cotton Bowl Christmas card from Syracuse. I was very impressed. I remember thinking that's where Roger went to school. I had watched the game and Jim Brown scored all those points. I thought, this guy Brown is some ball player. So I go up there to visit and they say, 'Roger's going to end up being an All-American.' I thought 'wow,' I played with this guy in high school. I should be able to at least make the team. They offered me a scholarship and I said yes. Here was a school that had gone to a couple of Bowl games plus I could get an engineering degree. There was no interference about that at all. In fact, part of my scholarship was based on academics."

KEN ERICSON (End): "After high school I received an appointment to West Point. I played football on the plebe team, my first year there. The Syracuse freshmen team happened to be on our schedule. After the game I talked to Otis Godfrey. He was one of the Syracuse players that I knew from high school. Otis told me he really liked it at Syracuse. The coaches were great, he liked the school, and all the players got along fine. I had become unhappy at West Point and was considering going somewhere else. After talking to Otis my mind was made up and I ended up transferring to Syracuse."

JIM ANDERSON (Halfback): "I got out of high school and I weighed like 165 pounds so I went to this elite New England prep school for a year to put on some weight. I felt like a kid from the other side of the tracks there. I almost got thrown out for shooting at a basket that was behind me. I shot a foul shot behind my head. The headmaster raced to the court and accused me of ruining 200 years of tradition.

"Anyway, I led New England prep schools in scoring and a coach from Duke came up to take a look at me. I was now up to about 185 pounds. The Duke coach said, 'Were any other schools interested?' I said, 'Syracuse.' And he said, 'Son, go there.' He said, 'You can play there, you probably can't play at Duke.' True story."

The most heavily recruited athlete on the '59 team was Ernie Davis. Syracuse was aware of Ernie's talents following his sophomore year at Elmira Free Academy. Ben made many trips to Elmira over Ernie's high school career slowly convincing him of the advantages of going to Syracuse. Davis had over fifty scholarship offers from across the country including Notre Dame, Air Force and UCLA. Today, athletes of this magnitude receive hundreds of offers but in 1958 the recruiting wasn't as sophisticated as it is today. Also, in 1958, many schools weren't offering athletic scholarships to black athletes. Ernie was later quoted in the newspapers as saying of the recruiting period, "I had a lot of people talking to me but I guess they knew from the start where I was going. Once I thought I would like to go to Notre Dame but I figured I might get lost in the shuffle. Syracuse is close to home."

MAURY YOUMANS (Tackle): "Before Ernie came to Syracuse I was in Ben's office. He said to me. 'Maury, we've got a young man coming here next year from Elmira. When he comes on the field before a game, the whole stadium stands up and cheers him. He's going to be a great one for us.' Ben was right."

The reality was Syracuse was getting good tough kids in their program. The ex-paratrooper built much of his coaching philosophy on military principles. He wanted players who were athletic, tough, and in shape. It was his job after he got them to mold them into a well-disciplined team. Schwartzwalder understood the recruiting process and ultimately looked for the best athletes available versus recruiting position by position. It was very common that the majority of a Syracuse recruiting class was made up of running backs and ends rather than the slower-footed, centers, and tackles.

John BROWN

TACKLE

When I went to Syracuse, there weren't that many black athletes . . . or black students. I'm not saying that in a derogatory manner but it was just the experience of going into this unknown arena. Coming from Camden, New Jersey and then all of a sudden you had to make this college team. Everybody in high school feels as though he or she can play in college, but that's not necessarily so. There is a lot of trepidation when you are going out on the field and you see all these seniors and these big guys out there. Although you're big, you find out that they are twice as strong as you are. But that's not the only aspect of college. You have the social aspect. Here you are going into an area where at that time there are very few minorities. This puts a lot of pressure on you. You had the pressure of being one of the few minorities in the school itself, also being one of three minorities on the football team. You're eighteen years old and trying to adjust to going to college. All these factors that you had to face made it pretty tough.

"It was really tough initially. Then the guys over a period of time really embraced us. That made it really nice."

John Brown. Courtesy of Syracuse University Athletic Communications.

Dick Easterly against Maryland. Courtesy of Syracuse University Archives.

7

Maryland

Schwartzwalder, although happy with the play of Dave Sarette in the Kansas game, declined to name him as the starting quarterback for the upcoming Maryland contest.

BEN SCHWARTZWALDER: "Sarette played a good but streaky game. He was far better quarterbacking the second team than the first where he froze up a little. But we think he'll be okay. I liked Schwedes at both halfback and quarterback. He'll play with more confidence next week against Maryland."

Against Kansas Schwedes played solidly at quarterback, completing 5 of 6 passes for 40 yards and one touchdown. At halftime Schwartzwalder gave him the word that his quarterbacking days were about over.

GERHARD SCHWEDES (Halfback): "Ben had told me at halftime that my quarterback days were about over. Sarette could handle the job. I was happy. I was going back to my true position, right halfback. He said, 'I want you to start the second half, but I'll move the young kid in so don't worry about it."

Maryland had lost six games in 1958. Their new coach, Tom Nugent, had been hired away from Florida State to rebuild the once proud football tradition. In the early 1950s Maryland had been a perennial football power. The 1951 Maryland team went undefeated which included an upset win over number one ranked Tennessee in the Sugar Bowl. At that time, Bowl outcomes weren't considered in deciding who would be the mythical national champions, and as a result Tennessee was voted the top team in the nation. But just two years later, under head coach Jim Tatum, Maryland won the National Championship.

Tom Nugent's record at Florida State was 34–28–2. In 1958 his Seminoles had gone 7–4 and were invited to play in the Bluebonnet Bowl. Nugent was very creative, and his offensive strategies were ahead of their time. He had developed a completely new offense, which he called the "I-formation." All three of his backs would form a straight line behind the quarterback. Today, it is common to see teams operate out of the "I" but in 1959 it was innovative. Out of the "I," Maryland was able to run twenty-six different options. When his team was faced with third and long situations, Nugent, prior to the ball being snapped, would have his backs split as the quarterback dropped back seven yards. This formation had the look of the old double-wing used by teams in the 1920s and 1930s. Today it would be referred to as the "shotgun." Syracuse would have a lot of work to do to prepare for this team.

BEN SCHWARTZWALDER: "We'll have to spend an awful lot of time on defense this week getting ready for Maryland. I think Saturday's game will be a high scoring game."

Coach Bill Bell had been assigned to scout Maryland's second game of the season against the Texas Longhorns. Maryland had opened the '59 season by defeating West Virginia, 27–7. Maryland's quarterback, Richie Novak, had completed 11 out of 12 passes against the Mountaineers and appeared to have the talent to carry his team to a winning season.

On the game's second play against Texas Novak sprained his ankle. Although he stayed in the contest, Novak was largely ineffective. Texas beat Maryland, 26–0. His availability for the upcoming game against Syracuse became the story line during the week. Novak's ankle also got considerable talk and concern from both coaches. At the beginning of the week, Nugent said, "Novak is definitely out for the Syracuse game." Realizing that he was making it too easy for Syracuse by declaring his starting quarterback out, he backtracked saying, "Novak *proba-bly* won't play." Schwartzwalder would have none of it and prepared to face the Terrapin's with their starting quarterback.

Maryland had a young assistant coach on it's staff by the name of Lee Corso. Corso had graduated from Florida State in 1957 and had planned to coach high school football. Tom Nugent intervened and offered him a graduate assistant's position at Florida State. Corso accepted Nugent's offer and turned his sights towards becoming a college football coach. When Nugent moved onto Maryland he brought Corso with him.

LEE CORSO (ESPN Football Commentator): "Tom Nugent invented the 'I-formation.' He brought it to Florida State and I was his first 'I-formation' quarterback there. I thought I was going to go to Miami but Tom Nugent changed my mind. He came in and talked to me about the principles that he believed in. I had great faith in him. Also he wanted me to come to Florida State and be a part of building the program, rather than maintaining one, like it would be in Miami at that time. I followed him to Maryland as one of his assistants."

The Syracuse press continued to badger Schwartzwalder about who would start at quarterback, Schwedes or Sarette? Ben, always trying to get an edge over the opponent, didn't want to tip his hand. "First," he said, "it depends if Mark Weber's healthy." Realizing the press wasn't buying into that statement, he then told the press, "All I can tell you is Schwedes will start somewhere in the backfield."

On Saturday, October 3, 1959, the Maryland football team showed up at Archbold Stadium without their starting quarterback, Richie Novak. Novak's severely sprained ankle did not respond to treatment and the young quarterback, on crutches, took a seat on the sidelines. Tom Nugent was forced to go with his backup quarterback, Dick Scarbath.

Nugent, whose "I-formation" was being hailed by other college coaches around the country as brilliant, got a dose of reality this day. He, like so many of his brethren coaching football, quickly discovered that you don't win with the tricky plays, you win with the right players.

Syracuse dominated Maryland from the opening kickoff to the final gun. No other Syracuse team in school history had ever dominated another team so badly. In beating Maryland 29–0, the Orangemen never allowed the 'Terps' to cross midfield. Led by its strong front line, Syracuse scored three of it's four touchdowns off forced turnovers by Maryland.

In the first quarter, Syracuse's top lineman, Roger Davis, sacked Maryland's quarterback Scarbath for a nine-yard loss, forcing the Terrapins to punt. Davis then blocked the ensuing punt, setting up the game's first score, a 25-yard field goal, by Bob Yates.

Syracuse held Maryland to a total of 29 yards in total offense. Nugent's team gained 8 yards rushing and 21 yards passing. Syracuse racked up 19 first downs compared to Maryland's two. Syracuse had gained 338 yards in total offense.

The Orange's passing game, directed by (starting) quarterback Dave Sarette, was only 6–19 for 50 yards. The problem was the Syracuse receivers who did a poor job of catching the ball. Syracuse had only one sustained drive for the entire game, a 67-yard drive finished off by a 26-yard touchdown run off the "scissors play" by Ernie Davis. The sophomore halfback gained 77 yards on 13 carries. Gerhard Schwedes, now back at his familiar right halfback position, added 70 yards on 8 carries.

TOM NUGENT (Maryland Head Coach): "Syracuse has more size and equipment than any team we have faced thus far. Texas has the better backs but Syracuse has the better overall balance. They have the horses. They are a very good football team."

BEN SCHWARTZWALDER: "We won the game and you can't get so hungry that you don't appreciate a win against any team, but we made every mistake in the book (three turnovers). We really had a letdown on offense in the second half, but with sophomore quarterbacks you can't expect them to play like seniors. I was certainly proud of our defense, especially Roger Davis, Bob Stem and Dick Fiedler."

Syracuse, in two games, had racked up 51 first downs to the opponent's 6. They had outgained the first two foes in total offense, 831 yards to 96 yards.

LEE CORSO (ESPN Football Commentator): "In 1959 I can remember walking into Archbold Stadium and feeling like the gladiators at the Coliseum. It was all concrete seats and it was like a bowl. It was really scary. Syracuse came out and they just literally killed us. In the fourth quarter we finally got a first down and the entire student body stood up and gave us a standing ovation. We used everything against them and we still couldn't move the football."

Following the game the players were elated with the win. Schwedes was happy to be back at his true position, running back. Big Gene Grabowski celebrated his first ever touchdown. The 6'5", 250-pound tackle fell on the loose pigskin in the end zone for the only score of the second half. Grabowski would make a couple of more huge plays for the Orangemen before this season was over.

Two players though had something very special planned for the evening. Bob Yates and his roommate Al "Jack" Bemiller were going to ask their girlfriends to marry them.

BOB YATES (Tackle): "Al Zak (equipment manager) took us down to some jeweler and got us two rings. We had it planned that we would go to this Italian restaurant on Salina Street after the Maryland game and propose to our girlfriends."

AL BEMILLER (Center): "We're sitting at this restaurant eating and both of us go back to the men's room, just like two girls would go back to the bathroom together. We had this all lined up that both of us were going to get engaged together. So we went back there and we were just bullshitting. I said, 'Okay buddy, you go first.' We come out and Yates made this big spiel to his girl, 'I love you, please be my wife forever,' and bla bla bla, . . . everything like that. After he was finished, I said, 'And the same goes for me.' My wife and I have been together ever since."

Syracuse Staff 1959 (left to right): Ben Schwartzwalder, Bill Bell, Ted Dailey, Rocco Pirro, Roy Simmons, Joe Szombathy, and Jim Shreve. Courtesy of Syracuse University Archives.

The Staff

"You win with people," was how legendary Ohio State Coach Woody Hayes explained his successful coaching career. Ben Schwartzwalder, in building his own successful football program at Syracuse, did just that, but what Ben did, which few head coaches are able to do, was keep the core of his assistant coaches intact. Rocco Pirro, Roy Simmons, Ted Dailey, and Bill Bell were with Schwartzwalder almost his entire time at Syracuse. In a business where most assistants work towards someday becoming the head coach, these men were content to stay with Schwartzwalder.

GERHARD SCHWEDES (Halfback): "I really think none of the '59 coaches wanted to ever leave Ben, or Syracuse, They were all hometown folks. I mean they were the guys you met in the local bar, they were together years, this was their home, this was there comfort zone. None of them wanted to leave. If Ben decided he wanted to coach somewhere else he would have had a tough time getting any of them to go. I don't think any of them would have left."

JIM SHREVE (Freshmen Coach): "Everybody enjoyed working with him so much. They loved Syracuse, they loved the area. They wanted to raise their families there. I'm not sure how many really tried to get out during those days to tell you the truth."

Rocco Pirro

IDA PIRRO: "I was at Syracuse and he was at Catholic University, and on one of my double dates, I met Rock's sister. We went back to her house and she showed me pictures of her two brothers. She told me that they both were going to school at Catholic University. One picture was of Rock and the other picture was of his brother Carmen who later was lost in the war. I said that he was cute. Well, the next thing I know he's at one of my softball games. I could see him on the sidelines. He came to all my games but never spoke to me until the last game.

"We had a kind of a 'old home day' and we all came to the game in trucks. When the truck stopped and I got off, he was standing right there, so I said, 'Hello.' The next day his buddy called me and invited me to a farewell party for Rock. He was going back to college the next day. Rock, being so shy, had his friend call me. That started it, then we both went into the service. We were married in the service in 1944. I ended up being stationed in Washington. He was at Bainbridge, Maryland. It took me a couple of months to file for a discharge and then I joined him. He ended up getting orders to go to Fleet City, California to play football and of course, I went with him.

"While we were out there the manager of the Buffalo Bisons, of the newly formed All-American League came calling. He was out there to sign up these ball players. I remember we had a Quonset hut and this guy wanted to sign all the ball players in our hut, so he gave me a hundred dollars to go to the track and basically get lost. I said to Rock,'Don't you sign anything until you talk to me. I don't know if I want to go to Buffalo.'

"When I came back he said, 'We all signed. They gave us bonuses!' Each guy who signed got a $500 dollar bonus. All the players thought that was the greatest thing that ever happened to them. Of course, in those days that was lot of money. We were in Buffalo four years before the team moved to Cleveland and became the Cleveland Browns. The Buffalo coach, Clem Crowe, went to the Baltimore team and took Rock with him. That was Rock's first year coaching.

"While that was happening, Ben gets the job at Syracuse. I told

Rock to write him a letter. 'Tell him you're looking for a job.' Rock said, 'Oh, he's got his staff.' I said, 'Write him a letter anyway.'

"So, he wrote him a letter, then after another year Ben called him. He said that one of his coaches left and he had an opening. He said Rock has been on his mind all that time and that's how we ended up in Syracuse."

MAURY YOUMANS (Tackle): "If Bill Bell played the bad guy, Rock played the other side. He was always the good guy that was going to help you, and did. If there was a problem, Rock would resolve it for you. You felt comfortable going to Rock. You knew that if something had to be said in confidence, Rock would keep it that way, so there was just a great trust factor. Also, he was local being from Solvay. He knew everybody in town. If you had a situation that you needed to get resolved, Rock could take care of it. I think Rock was a good coach, much better in hindsight than I thought during the time I played there. He used a lot of psychology. But you see, Rock had played football. You had a lot of respect for a guy who had been in the trenches."

DICK EASTERLY (Quarterback): "Rocco Pirro was loved by everybody, particularly if you didn't play for Rock, you know, he could kid a lot with you. Rocco lived in Solvay, but he could be one of the guys. He used to come down to my house down on Wolf street and play poker with a couple of the ball players. My dad and my brothers would go out to dinner and Rock knew I didn't have any money so he would slip me a couple of bucks. Later on, after I graduated, when I would see Rock, each time he would always open up with, 'There's that guy, Easterly, that took the option out of the option play.' Rock was the coach that kept everybody together. Rock was a good guy."

AL GERLICK (Tackle): "Rock used to love to tease me. One day he said, 'Gerlick, you're all balls and no cannon, Cannonball.' The name stuck."

LEON CHOLOKIS (Tackle): "One time Rocco lined up against me as a defensive end. He just kicked the shit out of me when I was supposed to block him. He had the strongest forearms. He was strong plus he was a good athlete. When you played four-wall handball against him, you did all the running. The man would move three steps. He'd have you running all over the court."

JERRY SKONIECZKI (End): "I remember when we were playing home games we each would get a couple of tickets, and me being from Binghamton, would always need more tickets. I'd ask all the guys from Boston, New Jersey, all those places, you going to use your tickets? Rock hears me, and says, 'Skonieczki, who the hell you bringing in here? You got to be selling these tickets.' I said, I'll replace them. When we go on the road I'll give the tickets to the guys.

"We're on the road, eating lunch, and Rock stands up and says, 'Who wants Skonieczki's tickets?' He wasn't going to let me get away with nothing. I loved that man."

JOE SZOMBATHY (Assistant Coach): "Rock, he would get calls at home and he would come in the next day and say, 'Damn it, I got a call at two o'clock in the morning.' He'd growl and bitch a little bit. Rock was the guy that would call on the local guy who knew everybody to stop any uprising.

"Rock was a hell of a ball player in his own right. He was captain of the Buffalo bills. He was a tough son-of-a-gun in his time."

JERRY SKONIECZKI (End): "When we were underclassmen I used to give Bob Yates a hard time. I'd call him a 'candy ass,' or a 'pussy.' So one day Rock says during practice, 'Okay, let's have the ends and backs over here, guards and tackles over there.' I start running over with my group, the ends and backs. Rock yells, 'Skonieczki, you go with the guards and tackles.' We proceeded to play "bull in the ring." You would form a circle with one player in the middle, the players around the circle would have a number. The coaches would call out a number, and that player whose number is called would try to knock the guy in the ring down and vice versa. Well, Rock puts me in the middle and proceeds to call out one number only, Yates, over and over. He got even that day. He just cleaned my clock. I have said ever since, I was responsible for turning him into an All-American football player."

Roy Simmons

GERHARD SCHWEDES (Halfback): "Roy Simmons was probably the best analyst I was ever around. When he came back after scouting our next opponent, he knew exactly what our game plan should be.

He knew who we should attack. He knew what our weaknesses were against the other teams and what we should do to prevent it. Roy Simmons was absolutely phenomenal. Simmons was the guy at halftime of games who was up on the chalkboard. He would explain the adjustments our team needed to make in the second half. Also, when he told you things, you believed him."

DICK EASTERLY (Quarterback): "Roy Simmons was a terrific coach. He would give you credit if you made a good play or not. Roy wasn't with us that much during games because he would be scouting next week's opponent. Roy Simmons was always interesting. When he came back from scouting he would give us the scouting report. Well, I want to tell you every team we played, including the Colgate Red Raiders according to Roy, were probably better than the Green Bay Packers. He sure would get you ready and he had a vocabulary all his own. He was a very interesting man. It was particularly fun for me being a defensive back to be coached by him. He was a hitter himself when he played, a tough guy, and he was from the old school. That guy was one great defensive back coach.

"He always wanted me to play lacrosse but I told him no because I loved baseball too much. He'd say,'You got to play for me,' but I didn't. He kept after me, though, because he liked certain types of guys for his players and he wouldn't take no for an answer."

JIM SHREVE (Freshmen Coach): "Roy Simmons was never in our meetings. He coached two other sports, boxing and lacrosse. He would come and coach the defensive backfield right off the top of his head."

DICK BEYER (Assistant Coach): "Simmy and I would scout together. We would leave on Friday and go scout Army, Holy Cross, Pitt, whoever we were playing next week. We would come back and we would present our scouting report on Sunday nights to the whole team. We would go over offensive plays that they were going to run. We would go over the other guy's defense. We would get into personnel, this guy's tough, this guy's not so tough. Like Mike Ditka, we had, 'He's a head hunter. Don't turn your back on him.' It was fun and I learned a lot from Simmy.

"In the mid-1950s when I was wrestling professionally, Simmy used to love it when we would go away on a scouting trip and I could work it in to wrestle. He would say, 'Are you wrestling this weekend?' I'd say, 'Buffalo.' He says, 'Great, I'll be in your corner.' It was funny, it was like he thought I was boxing and needed someone in my corner. Anyway, he says, 'You wrestle in Buffalo at eight-thirty, we can get to Erie by ten and watch the Friday night fights.' The next morning we would go down to Pitt and scout the game and then we would drive back to Syracuse."

JERRY SKONIECZKI (End): "Roy Simmons once said to me after a film session, 'Skonieczki, you are neither hay nor grass.' I was playing defensive end and I get caught in that twilight zone: Is it a run or a pass? Sometimes you don't know, right? And I'm staying right in the middle. Simmons correctly says, 'You got to make a commitment one way or the other because you got linebackers to take over for you if you go after the quarterback.' Later I thought,'How prophetic: I'm neither hay nor grass. He was right."

Ted Dailey

THELMA DAILEY: "When Ted graduated from Pittsburgh, he played a year with the Steelers. That was only a part-time job in those days. He decided he needed a permanent job with a salary coming in, something he could rely on, so he went to Coatesville in southeastern Pennsylvania. It was a steel town and he was a very popular coach. He won a lot of games and the people there have never forgot him. They have a picture of him hanging at the school and he's in their Hall Of Fame.

"Ted was an end at Pittsburgh and played in the Rose Bowl against Southern Cal. There was an article in a New York paper. At the time Richard Nixon was running for President, he made the statement that Pitt didn't win the Rose Bowl that year 'but there was a little end by the name of Ted Dailey who he never will forget. He was quite a player for his size, the best player in the game.' Ted wrote Nixon back and said, 'Anybody that remembers that far back deserves my vote.' He received later in the mail, a nice note from Mr. Nixon and a picture of his family."

MAURY YOUMANS (Tackle): "Probably the guy that was most

Ted Dailey, Starting End,
University of Pittsburgh,
circa 1932. Courtesy of
Thelma Dailey.

outstanding to me as a coach was Ted Dailey. Ted liked defense. He liked hard hitting. I made a tackle on a punt return right in front of the bench. I punished this guy. I really hit him, knocked him out. Ted really liked that. I remember he made a comment about it. I just had a lot of respect for him. Most of the players were close with Rock Pirro. I was too. I liked Rock a lot. But I thought if you're going to take a stance in a situation, Ted was the guy who was going to take one. We had Les Dye as a freshman coach and he was pretty tough, but Ted was tougher, and he knew how to make you a better player. He got the best out of you."

JOE SZOMBATHY (Assistant Coach): "He was a very good football player, one of the early guys to get a scholarship to college to play football. He also was one of the first guys to play in the Rose Bowl and that used to piss Rocco Pirro off. Ted used to brag about it, 'Well we played in the Rose Bowl, got beat 35–0.' Rock, he stutters, 'What good was that? You got your ass beat!' Ted was a great defensive coach."

DICK EASTERLY (Quarterback): "Now you take Ted Dailey. If you were any good he would tell you, and if you weren't any good, he'd tell you that too. He called a spade a spade."

FRED MAUTINO (End): "Ted Dailey was a tough coach. He would never fail to remind you if you had done something wrong."

Bill Bell

"I first started playing for Ben in high school in West Virginia. I had met him when he came down to Parkersburg in 1937. I played for him in 1938 and in 1939. Things were a lot different then, a little slower. Competitive wise, just the same. We played just as hard but not quite as fast. The running game was always the main thing with Ben. Being tough was always there. We didn't have the emphasis back then on the strength and the bulk, you know, as it is now. I remember the first weights I ever saw. Ben brought them into our old wrestling room in high school. It was just an old darn bar. There were two concrete boxes on the end of them. I thought, you know, what the hell are these things? And that was the first I saw of any kind of weights. Ben was always a big one for rope climbing. You know, up the rope? Everyone had to scale the ropes. That was one of our conditioning things.

"After I came back from the service he had just gotten the job at Muhlenberg College in Allentown, Pennsylvania. I was home, planning on going back up to West Virginia University. I was there when the war broke out and I had planned to return after the war, finish my education, and play football. I had played my first two years prior to the war at Morgantown. Ben wanted me to come up and play for him and I was happy to go. I played two years for Ben up at Muhlenberg College. I started out as a tailback in the single wing. I had hurt my knee and couldn't run too well so Ben started fooling with the "T-formation," putting me up under the center. I ended up running the offense we had up at Syracuse which included the unbalanced line.

"When I left college at Muhlenberg, I was drafted by the San Francisco 49ers. In fact, I was looking at my old contract just the other day here at home. I got a $2,000 bonus and a $7,000 contract. I thought, 'My God, that's more money than there is in the world.'

"So I went out to the 49ers in 1948. Frankie Albert was the quarterback. Frankie was supposed to be retiring because, physically, he was having trouble playing. Buck Shaw was coaching and that's the only reason I went out there. I figured I had a chance at playing if they didn't have a real good quarterback. I got out there and Frankie came back and looked strong. I thought, 'My God, look at these guys.' I was out there with Albert at quarterback and all these players I had read about. I lasted part of the preseason, then they cut me. I came back to Ohio and took a job as assistant coach at Marietta College. Ben at this time had just gotten the Syracuse job. He was attending a coaching clinic in Charleston, West Virginia and I ran into him there. I got talking to him and he asked me if I wanted to come up and work with him and go to school. I still had some of the GI bill left so I said, 'yes.' That's how I got up there. He understood me and I understood him. We were thinking alike in our approach to football. That's how it happens."

MAURY YOUMANS (Tackle): "Bill Bell was a kind of a black and white kind of guy. Either you liked him or you didn't like him. There wasn't any gray area in between. Some coaches, like Tom Landry who I played for at Dallas, are easy going, more intellectual. They don't get into yelling and stuff like that. Some coaches need a yeller. Ben really didn't need a yeller but I think, if anything, Bill could play the bad guy for Ben. Every coach needs somebody that's going to do that."

Joe Szombathy

"I was teaching at a high school and coaching football in Pennsylvania when they offered me the assistant's job at Syracuse in 1957. They offered me $4,800 dollars. I jumped. I said, 'Are you kidding me?' I was at the time making $3,500 dollars a year. I was on cloud nine. Lou Andreas was the athletic director. He said,'You got to move up here.'I asked, 'Well, how much you gonna give me to move?' Andreas, always the tightwad, says, 'We'll give you $250 dollars.'

They gave me a lot of responsibility right off. I was going to be a recruiter and coach on the field, but my main job was to make sure everybody remained eligible. I'd sit in on meetings at the end of each semester when they reviewed each players eligibility.

"Regarding that first year, I hadn't moved up to Syracuse yet. It's July and I get a phone call from Ben,'We're going to have a meeting to start getting ready for the season,' he says. 'I want you up here August 1.' 'Holy cow,' I said. 'August first. I got nowhere to stay.' Ben says, 'Don't worry, we'll find a place for you. Get up here.' The first day I arrived the whole staff was wined and dined by old Blaine Clark, an alumni who owned the Clark Trucking Company. They had a big party as his place. I think we ended up playing cards. The next morning, bright and early, we were in meetings and Ben was at the chalkboard."

DAVE BAKER (End): "My favorite coach was Joe Szombathy. He was my end coach. Joe was a good guy. He treated me very well."

FRED MAUTINO (End): "Joe was a young coach at that time, not much older than the players, and we could relate to him. He was a good coach and we formed a tight bond."

Al Zak

BRUCE HOAG (Senior Manager): "Al always appeared to be hard but Al had a heart of gold. He was probably a softie more than he was hard. His hardness toward the players I think was a defense. He cared about everybody."

BILL RAPP, JR. (Student Manager): "Oh my goodness, he scared the crap out of me; just the name itself still does. You were scared because you heard stories about him coming in as a freshman. Bruce Hoag was the senior manager and Bruce said, 'You'd better do everything he tells you to do or you're out of here on your ass.' The first time you meet him he was just so gruff and rough. He scared a lot of the scholarship players as well as freshmen managers. I think some of the upperclassmen maybe got to know him a little better, but the fresh-

Al Zak circa 1930's. Courtesy of Syracuse University Archives.

men players would come in and he would stand there yelling at them. There would be Julie Richel (head trainer) on one side with Neil Pratt (assistant trainer) and Al Zak on the other side. The poor players had to walk right between them to get to the lockers. He would like to yell at them, 'You dumb frosh!' And if you misplaced a sock or something, Lord help you. I think even Ernie Davis got yelled at. Ernie forgot to turn in one of his socks or something one time.

"He wanted everything perfect inside that equipment room. Everything had to be exactly right. We had to match everything. The managers before the games set everything up for the players. Everything had to be absolutely perfect, I mean he was a tough task man. When I was an upperclassmen he was a lot easier on me. Later on he became a very good car customer of mine. He and Ellen would come in and buy cars. We got to be good friends."

DICK BEYER (Assistant Coach): "Al Zak, he was a horse of another color. He was tough to get to know. You know, you couldn't get socks, you couldn't get a jock. If you wore it in the morning and it was sweaty like hell, he'd say, 'Ya get one in da morning and that's it! You dumb shit.' That never changed."

LEON CHOLOKIS (Tackle): "His bark was worse than his bite, that's for sure. Anytime you needed a favor or anything he was always there to give it to you."

BOB STEM (Center): "I'm coming off the field and somebody rips my chin strap off so I go see Al Zak. I told him somebody took my chin strap. He said, 'You Goddamn dumb sophomore, here's 35 cents, take a bus to Colgate.' He would not give me a Goddamn chin strap. I went and told Ben. I said, 'Al Zak won't give me a chin strap.' So Ben brings me in and says, 'Ok, Al, Bobby needs a chin strap and you're going to take care of him, right?' He gave me a chin strap. That's the only way I would have got a chin strap from the guy."

DAVE BAKER (End): "Al Zak? Christ, we tried to steal as much as we could from him. We got these new socks for every game. I'd wear an old pair in the games and take the new socks and wear around campus. Al Zak was a good guy, he was."

GERHARD SCHWEDES (Halfback): "Al Zak's favorite word was, 'Dumb Shit,' but he was a real, real cog in our '59 team. When they made me captain I made him a part of the '59 team. Before games I would ask him to say something to the team. He would use some simple cliches but nothing more than three word sentences. That was Al. He spoke before every game before we went out on the field."

MAURY YOUMANS (Tackle): "Al Zak never bothered me like he did a lot of guys. He loved to call everybody a 'Dumb Shit.' It was just his way. I guess in my freshman year you were a 'dumb frosh.' After that, you were a 'Dumb Shit.'"

KEN ERICSON (End): "That man chased me for two years because he said I didn't turn in a shirt. He finally threatened to take my meal ticket away if he didn't get it back. He was something else."

FRED MAUTINO (End): "He would put on this big show about being tough but he loved the players. He was a great guy. He bled Orange, that's for sure."

Julie Reichel

BILL RAPP, JR. (Student Manager): "Julie was quiet and he was a very good friend of Ben and Ted Dailey. The kids trusted him and the coaches trusted him. Everybody had confidence in what he said. If he said you couldn't play, you couldn't play. Tough as Ben was, if Julie said, 'This is the way it is,' that's the way it was.

"I remember one time on the sidelines during the 1959 Orange Bowl (1958 season, 1959 Orange Bowl). I remember Jim Lamey getting hurt. He had a broken leg as it turned out but nobody knew it. He came out and he told Coach, 'I can't walk,' and he turned to go sit down. Schwartzwalder pushed him back in and said, 'Get your ass back in there and make a tackle.' He played as it turned out, half the game with a broken leg. That didn't happen very often because Julie was good and Ben trusted him. Ben may not have liked it when Julie said a kid couldn't play, but almost always, Ben would go along with the decision."

BRUCE HOAG (Senior Manager): "Julie probably was the toughest one for me to get along with. He gave some misdirection a couple of times which put me in an uncomfortable position. Fortunately I had a good enough relationship with the coaches I just went and said, 'Hey, this is what he said, this is what I did, so you figure out what you want done.' "

Doc Barney

LEON CHOLOKIS (Tackle): "My freshman year my ankle was swollen and he told me it was water on my knee. It had swelled around my ankle and Dr. Barney says, 'I'm going to drain it.' He put one of those big fucking hypodermic needles with the square needle on it to draw out the water. Blood comes out so I freak and I say, 'That's blood coming out!' And he says, 'Well, blood has water in it.'

"We all wanted to get out of spring practice, so what I used to do was go down and brush my teeth and I'd swallow the toothpaste. Then I would go to him and tell him I had a sore throat. He would tell me to open my mouth and he'd say, 'Oh, your tonsils are terrible. They're all white and pussy.' I did that two or three days in a row. After the '59 season, he says,'In the summertime we'll have to get em out.' And they took my fuckin tonsils out! I couldn't say no."

MAURY YOUMANS (Tackle): "We were practicing actually for the Cotton Bowl and Roger Davis had either the flu or just a really bad cold. Doctor Barney told Roger that he had to have a shot of penicillin. Well, Roger told him where he could put his shot; he wasn't going to get one. Doc Barney was bound and determined to give him that shot. We had finished practice and I was at my locker. I was stripping off my football gear and I had bent over to pick something up. All of a sudden, 'Wham,' I felt a stinging in my butt. I turned around and Doc Barney says, 'I got you.' He thought he had Roger Davis. He gave me a big shot in the butt. Obviously, I didn't catch a cold for the rest of the year."

TOM GILBURG (End): "One of Doc Barney's favorite sayings was, 'If you hit yourself in the head with a hammer, it feels good when you stop.'

"You'd go back and tell him one story and he'd come back with twenty stories. On the sidelines during the Colgate game, old Doc Barney was saying, 'Come on guys, five more points and you've got my age.' "

BOB STEM (Center): "One of the guys cuts his leg in practice and it's bleeding pretty good. My knee was a little swollen at the time so I wasn't doing much in practice. Ben says,'Listen Stemmy, you walk him in, make sure he gets in there okay.' So I walked in with him. We were both dressed in football uniforms but I don't have my helmet on. I said, 'Doc, this guy's bleeding pretty bad.' He looks up and he says, 'Yeah, what sport you in?' I said, standing there in my uniform,'Football, we're football players.' "

KEN ERICSON (End): "I had a bad back and I went to him for treatment. I remember he said, 'Kid, you might as well get used to it. You're going to have it the rest of your life.' He was right."

Bruce HOAG

SENIOR MANAGER

I was either going to do something with the football team or I was probably going to transfer to another college, it wasn't a place I felt I was part of. If I didn't do something with football, I would have been a student walking around doing nothing.

"My responsibilities during the season were to take care of all the players. Make sure there was water, and footballs, practice tees, whatever else they needed. Everything was there that was supposed to be there, general student manager type junk.

"The training staff on game day had to be up at 5:00 am, and be down to the stadium getting ready, while the players were still sleeping. We had to make sure all the equipment was available. On game day you had to make sure all the uniforms were out and everything is clean and hung up. Everything had to be in the right place so when the players walked in they could concentrate on what they had to do, rather than search for stuff.

"On Sundays I drove down to Ithaca to get all the game films developed. There was no Interstate 81 then so you had to go Route 11 down through Cortland, all the way down to Ithaca. That was no little chore. I'd take off on a Sunday morning and be in Ithaca all day waiting for the film to be developed. I would then bring them back for the coaches so they could look at them Sunday night.

"My relationship with the players was different than I think other managers typically have. The players were more my friends. I lived with them, we did things together where other managers usually don't.

"I used to go over and have coffee with the Schwartzwalders' on weekends. I was always welcome there. I became a surrogate type person with their family, who could go over any time I wanted to. I don't know if a lot of people knew how very, very dear people they were."

"Game concentration." Left to right: Ted Dailey, Rocco Pirro, and Ben
Schwartzwalder. Courtesy of Thelma Dailey.

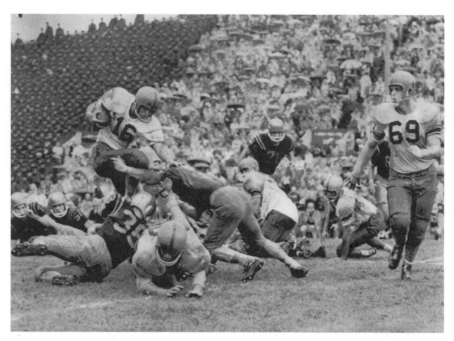

Gerhard Schwedes goes over the top against Navy. Courtesy of Gerhard Schwedes.

Navy

The Lambert Trophy, awarded to the top Eastern college team, was a big deal in 1959. Competition between all the Eastern schools was great, with Penn State, Army, and Navy still viable opponents. The Nittany Lions were playing a predominately Eastern schedule and the Service Academies were still able to recruit top athletes. Each week, in addition to the national polls, the Eastern newspapers published the standings in the Lambert Trophy race, a mythical standings that meant something to each school's fans.

Following its massacre of Maryland, Syracuse moved up to the top spot in the East. Undefeated Penn State was second followed by Navy, Army and Pittsburgh, respectively. Syracuse, an early three point favorite over Navy in this week's Oyster Bowl (Norfolk, Virginia), was ranked twelfth nationally by the Associated Press and eleventh by the United Press International. The Orangemen, who were now leading the country in three defensive categories—total defense, rushing defense and passing defense—still could not crack the Top Ten. Pittsburgh's head coach, John Michelson, was outraged by the snub of the Orangemen and Eastern football.

JOHN MICHELSON (Pittsburgh Head Coach): "Syracuse has one of the best teams in all of college football. They clearly are the most underrated team in America."

Navy came into the Syracuse game with a record of 2–1. Easily defeating Boston College and William and Mary in their first two games, the Midshipmen moved up in class the previous week playing nationally ranked SMU on the road. The Middies, trailing 14–7 with two minutes to go in the game, had a first down just inside SMU's 10-yard line. Attempting to pass, the ball was intercepted at the line of scrimmage by the Mustangs and returned ninety-five yards for a touchdown. Navy had dominated the statistics but three costly turnovers proved to be too much to overcome in a 20–7 loss. Syracuse's scout Joe Szombathy felt Navy would be the first true test for Syracuse.

First year coach Wayne Hardin felt overall his first and second teams played with equal skill. His first team, led by quarterback Joe Tranchini, an All-America candidate, and 5'10" running back Joe Bellino, probably were the better offensive unit. This pair of athletes presented opposing teams a very diverse challenge. Tranchini, an accurate passer, would throw twenty-five to thirty passes per game, while Bellino, one year away from winning the Heisman Trophy, was an extremely quick back with outstanding open field moves. After three games Bellino was averaging 8.9 yards per carry. He had injured his leg the previous Saturday in the SMU game and was questionable for the coming game. Schwartzwalder again took the high road and prepared his team as though Bellino was playing.

Many sportswriters across the country were picking Navy to beat Syracuse. New York's syndicated football prognosticator, Will Grimsley had Navy winning 18–7.

While the Orangemen prepared for Navy, the New York State Fair Board announced a plan to build a 60,000 seat stadium at the Fairgrounds in Syracuse with a projected cost of three million dollars. The Board hoped this brand new structure could replace old Archbold stadium as the home for the Syracuse football team. Syracuse's athletic director, Lew Andreas, when asked about the new stadium, said he had not been in contact with the State Fair Board. He reported that the last time he met with the Board there was a great discrepancy in the figures. This idea lasted a few months before it died a quick death. It became clear that if any stadium or facility was going be built for Syracuse football, it was going to be built on University property.

Syracuse's halfback, Mark Weber, just couldn't get healthy after being banged up in the last scrimmage prior to the start of the season. At times Syracuse's best back in the preseason, the 6'1" speedster from Solon, Ohio, was tired of watching from the sidelines. Like Navy's Bellino, he was listed as questionable for the game. Schwartzwalder hoped Weber would be available on Saturday, as he was a tough defender and Navy looked like a very difficult team to defend against.

BEN SCHWARTZWALDER: "This is quite a Navy football team. They have better speed and a better passing attack than anything we have seen this year. What's more, this is no small Navy team. They have a pair of tackles that are big as well as good. Both boys go about 230 pounds."

Foreman Field in Norfolk, Virginia was the home of The Oyster Bowl. The bowl game was founded by The Shriners in 1946 to raise money for crippled children. Each year the game sold out to capacity, 31,500. Through the 1958 game more than $570,000 had been raised. A unique twist was that a ticket was purchased for each person who entered Foreman Field that day. Boosters paid admission fees for the players and coaches from both teams, the referees, newsmen, everybody.

The weekend's festivity, which also included a big parade through downtown Norfolk, was held under rainy skies. Syracuse University's Band (One Hundred Men and a Girl) drove thirteen hours in a bus to perform in the parade and also at halftime of the game. On Friday morning the Syracuse football team flew into Norfolk on two charter planes. The team attended the kickoff luncheon, followed by a short forty-five-minute walk through Foreman Field. The Navy team, accompanied by its First Regiment, bused over from Annapolis. It was a big game for both teams.

Navy, like Maryland the week before, would play this game without one of their best players, Joe Bellino. His leg injury was far worse than anyone thought and the junior running back would watch from the sidelines.

The Midshipmen won the toss and elected to receive. Syracuse kicker Bob Yates teed up the ball under ugly, threatening skies to begin the thirteenth addition of the Oyster Bowl. The Middies, like Maryland before them, found out early the strength of Syracuse was its front line. Gaining just one yard on two carries, Navy quarterback Joe Tranchini, attempting to pass, was sacked by Syracuse's defensive end Fred Mautino. Navy was forced to punt. Ernie Davis fielded the ball at his own 34-yard line and the young sophomore returned the ball seven yards to give Syracuse good field position at their own 41-yard line. Syracuse went right to work. Quarterback Dave Sarette, starting his second straight game, found Mautino wide open at midfield for a 9-yard gain. Fullback Art Baker sliced off-tackle for four yards, picking up the Orangemen's initial first down. The field, soaked from the week of rain, aided the powerful Syracuse ground game as the Orange gained three and four yards at a time. Steadily moving down the field, Syracuse reached the Middies 3-yard line. On first down, halfback Schwedes was hit in the backfield and lost two yards. Two straight running plays netted four yards, setting up fourth down on the Navy 1-yard line. Schwartzwalder didn't hesitate. Yelling, "Let's go," he quickly signaled in the play. Syracuse broke the huddle setting their unbalanced line to the right with halfback Davis split out to the left. Sarette took the snap and turned to hand off to Baker, the big fullback charging forward toward a small space between guard Roger Davis and center Al Bemiller. Sarette faked a handoff to Baker, than tucking the ball in his arm, followed Baker into the pile. The Navy front line stiffened and the small hole closed. Baker, knees churning, saw Navy linebacker Jim Dunn in his path. The 205-pound fullback leaped into the air and hit Dunn in the chest, knocking the defender backward enough to allow Sarette to dive into the end zone. Yates' extra point was good and Syracuse led 7–0.

Schwartzwalder, following the kickoff, inserted his second unit. The second team, led by senior tackle Al Gerlick, had played well defensively in the first two games, but that wasn't to be today. Navy, starting from their own 20-yard line, marched down the field on a series of short passes and runs by halfback Joe Malavavage. On third and eight from Syracuse's 36-yard line, Navy ran a draw play with Malavavage sprinting eighteen yards to the Syracuse 18-yard line. Schwartzwalder had seen enough and he signaled his first team to go back in.

Navy continued to move the ball, pushing Syracuse's first unit back to the Orangemen's 6-yard line. There Tranchini, rolling out, was rushed by the entire Syracuse line led by Maury Youmans. Trying to avoid a sack he hurriedly threw toward a Navy receiver at the goal line. Baker, playing linebacker on defense, broke toward the receiver as Tranchini's arm started forward. Reaching out his arms, the extended Baker grabbed the ball at the 3-yard line. Now turning up the sideline, Baker saw only the Navy quarterback in his path. He wasn't there long. Bemiller, sprinting toward Tranchini, flattened him with a cross block that provided Baker clear sailing for a 97-yard touchdown run. The Oyster Bowl crowd, predominantly Navy fans, was stunned. Syracuse now led 13–0. Schwartzwalder decided to go for two. A Schwedes halfback pass was broken up in the end zone.

Navy's problems were just beginning as Syracuse created another turnover on the next series. The Middies, unable to move the ball, were forced to punt on fourth down. Gerlick broke through the line and blocked the punt allowing Mike Neary to recover at the 6-yard line. Syracuse had a golden opportunity to break the game wide open before halftime. Syracuse's second unit, back on the field, gained no yards on two running plays. Attempting to pass on third down, backup quarterback Dick Easterly was sacked for a 17-yard loss. Gerlick's 31-yard field goal attempt was wide right. Navy had dodged the bullet; they were still in the game.

The Midshipmen knew they needed to make something happen and mounted a strong drive. Behind Malavavage's strong running, they moved down the field, reaching the Syracuse 8-yard line. Again trying to pass with two Syracuse linemen in his face, Tranchini was picked off, this time by Ernie Davis at the 7-yard line. Syracuse, staying on the ground, moved the ball to the Navy 37-yard line. On first down, Sarette dropped back to pass, and spotting Schwedes wide open at the 19-yard line, gunned a perfect pass to his right halfback. Catching the ball in stride, Schwedes did the rest, outrunning the Navy defenders into the end zone for Syracuse's third touchdown. Yates' kick made it 20–0. Navy, on three tries, failed to move the ball and the first half came to a close.

At halftime the Syracuse coaching staff made sure the players didn't get overconfident and stressed the importance of keeping the pressure on the Navy quarterback. A big win against a quality opponent like Navy would help next week in the national polls.

Syracuse received the kickoff to start the second half and the Orange's big line continued to open huge holes in the Navy defense. The Middies just couldn't match up. At times the Middies resorted to using eight—and nine-men lines, but even that couldn't slow Syracuse's strong runners. Reaching the Middies 13-yard line, the Orange called on Baker. The big fullback broke through the line, cut to his left, then ran over one Navy defender as he rambles into the end zone. The fourteen play drive ate up over half of the third quarter. Schwartzwalder went for two again. Schwedes, starting right, reversed field twice trying to score. The senior ran almost sixty yards on the play in an effort to gain two yards but he was knocked out one yard short of the goal line. Syracuse now led 26–0.

In the fourth quarter Navy finally got on the scoreboard with an 18-yard pass from Tranchini to Malavavage. The try for two points failed when Syracuse defender Ed Bowers broke up the pass.

The last score of the day turned out to be one of the great plays in the history of Syracuse football. Navy completed a pass to receiver Jim Albershart. Albershart, turning to avoid being tackled by Mark Weber, was stripped of the ball. Like a thief in the night, Weber grabbed the pigskin and danced untouched into the end zone. No one could believe what they saw, especially the distraught Albershart who lay motionless on the field. Syracuse had stretched its lead to 32–6. Schwartzwalder, in love with the recently adopted two-point conversion concept, attempted it once again to no avail. Interestingly, back in 1959, college coaches became enamored with the two-point conversion but most still didn't have a real feel for when to use it. Because it was so new there was no accurate information available on its success rate. Unlike today, there were no charts to advise coaches when to go for two points. Many games played in the early days of the two-point conversion were lost by coaches greedily, 'going for two.'

Syracuse was now 3–0 and fullback Art Baker was voted the game's most valuable player. The junior back, in addition to his electrifying 97-yard interception, had gained 53 yards on 10 carries. Navy had fared better statistically than Syracuse's first two opponents. The Middies had gained 184 yards in total offense, 125 yards through the air and 59 yards on the ground. Syracuse gained 185 yards on the ground and 119 yards through passing. Syracuse was 7 of 10 passing, Navy was 10 of 28.

WAYNE HARDIN (Navy Head Coach): "By far this is the best team we've faced this year. Far better than Southern Methodist. These kids really hit."

JOE TRANCHINI (Navy Quarterback): "This Syracuse team is the best I've seen in any game against Navy in my four years at the Academy."

BEN SCHWARTZWALDER: "Navy is a tough team. I think they'll win their share of games from here on in. Our kids were up for this one and played a game they should be proud of."

Schwartzwalder was openly excited about his team's win calling it "A real team victory." His front lines again totally dominated the opposition. Navy quarterback Joe Tranchini was sacked five times for minus 28 yards. The only injury was to starting left end Jerry Skonieczski whose knee buckled in the fourth quarter after sacking Tranchini. Later in the locker room it was determined that his knee had just tightened up and he would be ready for Holy Cross next week. Syracuse was about to face the last team to defeat them in a regular season game. This time their coach vowed to have them ready to play.

Syracuse scores. Courtesy of Gerhard Schwedes.

10

Holy Cross

Dr. Eddie Anderson, the venerable head coach of football at the College of the Holy Cross in Worcester, Massachusetts, was a unique individual in the world of college football in the late fifties. When football season was over, he practiced medicine. He didn't get out his golf clubs or spend all his time on the road recruiting players. Instead he hung out his shingle and treated patients. Anderson, who in the fall of '59 was entering his 34th year coaching college football, was highly respected by his coaching peers. His teams were known for being well-prepared and playing aggressive football. Anderson, currently in his second tour of coaching the Crusaders, had beaten Syracuse the past two seasons. Last year's 14–13 upset by Holy Cross was the only loss during the regular season for the 1958 Orangemen. Ben Schwartzwalder was always concerned about facing a 'Dr. Eddie,' coached team.

Eddie Anderson was born in Oskaloosa, Iowa on November 13, 1900. A brilliant student in school, he was also an outstanding athlete playing three sports, his first love being football. Following his high school graduation, he entered Notre Dame and, as a freshman, was the starting end on the 1918 varsity football team. In his four years in South Bend, the Irish lost only one game. In his senior year Anderson earned All-America honors. Upon graduating from Notre Dame his coach, Knute Rockne, helped Anderson get into college coaching. His first coaching stint was at tiny Columbia College in Dubuque, Iowa. Next he moved to Depaul University in Chicago. While coaching football at Depaul, he earned his medical degree from Rush Medical School, somehow finding time to play professional football with the Chicago Cardinals.

Anderson became the head coach at Holy Cross in 1933. He coached there for six seasons, posting an impressive 47–7–4 record. His 1935 and his 1937 teams went undefeated. When the University of Iowa came calling in 1938 he couldn't refuse and returned home to coach the Hawkeyes. His 1939 team brought respectability back to Iowa football. Having lost only to Tom Harmon and Michigan 27–7, Iowa, in its last game, played Northwestern for a share of the Big Ten title. Crippled by injuries, the Hawkeyes fought to a 7–7 tie. Anderson was hailed throughout the state of Iowa for his team's outstanding season. A perennial doormat in the Big Ten, Iowa fans finally had something to cheer about.

Anderson, like Schwartzwalder, would resign his coaching position when the United States entered World War II. Enlisting in the Army, the doctor/coach spent three years overseas. Following the war Anderson returned to Iowa, and in 1950 the Iowa Athletic Board offered Anderson a new three-year contract. He asked that faculty tenure be included in the pact. When the Iowa board refused, Anderson resigned. Holy Cross, anxious to get Anderson back, immediately offered Anderson his old position. He accepted.

Anderson's 1959 Holy Cross team, going into the Syracuse game, was undefeated. Led by three-year starting guard Vince Promuto, the Crusaders had won three straight games to open the season. Holy Cross ranked second in the nation in rushing defense and seventh in total defense. But they had just lost starting quarterback Dick O'Brien to a ruptured kidney in last week's win over Dayton. The Crusaders would be the third team in a row to lose a key player to injury the week before meeting Syracuse.

Coach Anderson spent the early part of the week looking at three potential replacements before deciding on sophomore Bill Joern. Anderson felt Joern's ability to pass the ball better than the other two quarterbacks was the deciding factor. Junior running back Dick Skinner had been the main ball carrier for Holy Cross and now he would be counted on to carry the load against the nation's number one defense.

BEN SCHWARTZWALDER: "Don't sell Holy Cross short. They have the biggest team we will face all year. They will make us their objective this year."

EDDIE ANDERSON (Holy Cross Head Coach): "Syracuse is by far the best team we will meet this year. This is 'The Game of The Year,' for us. Syracuse's depth concerns me."

Syracuse, who had moved up to eighth in the national polls, was still ranked number one in the east, followed closely by undefeated Penn State. Holy Cross, unranked in the national polls, was ranked sixth in the East. Syracuse, based on strength of schedule, went into the game as a solid three-touchdown favorite.

Schwartzwalder, commenting on last week's Navy game, overall was pleased with his first unit's play but wasn't so kind to the second group.

BEN SCHWARTZWALDER: "Navy moved the ball pretty much at will against our seconds. Our second unit offense wasn't very good either. They had a first and goal at the six and couldn't score."

There would be very few negative comments made about the second group for the remainder of the season.

The Holy Cross team, warming up prior to the kickoff, was quite confident. The Crusaders had defeated Syracuse the past two years and they fully expected to play well today.

Early in the first period the men in purple shocked the Syracuse fans. Syracuse quarterback Dave Sarette slipped attempting a pitch out to Gerhard Schwedes and the ball popped into the air. Crusader defender Dick Skinner alertly snatched the ball and ran it 55 yards for a touchdown. Syracuse fans were aghast. Could upstart Holy Cross do the unthinkable and once again upset the Orange? Syracuse, who had won nine straight at Archbold Stadium, was again on the short end of the stick to Holy Cross. Eddie Anderson, sensing Syracuse's confusion on the surprise touchdown, went for two points on the conversion. Syracuse's Roger Davis crushed Skinner before he reached the line of scrimmage and Holy Cross lead stayed at 6–0.

Schwedes returned Bill Joern's kickoff to his own 34-yard line. Syracuse moved the ball into Holy Cross territory, but the Crusader defense held and forced Syracuse to punt. Schwartzwalder, at this point in the game, decided to substitute, putting his second team defense on the field. On third down from the Crusader 25, Joern hit left end Charlie Pacunas for eleven yards and a first down. Schwartzwalder, shaking his head on the sidelines, wondered if he was about to see a repeat of last week's poor performance by his second group. Syracuse, shifting defenses just prior to the snap, forced a fumble on the ensuing play and Syracuse tackle Leon Cholokis recovered at the Crusader 35-yard line. The Orange's second unit, behind the running of Whitey Reimer and Dick Anderson, moved the ball to the Holy Cross 14. On fourth and one, Syracuse went for it, attempting an off-tackle slant. Halfback Jim Anderson was held for no gain and Holy Cross took over on downs. The second team's defensive players, determined to make up for last week's poor play, gave up one first down before forcing Holy Cross to punt. Crusader punter Joern, taking the snap at his own 18, got off a poor punt and the ball came to rest just past the midfield stripe. This time, with great field position and the first unit back in the game, the sputtering Orange offense began to roll. Schwedes, taking a pitch from Sarette, ran 29 yards for a first down. Following a Holy Cross offside penalty, Sarette, off a play-action pass, hit Fred Mautino in the end zone for Syracuse's first score. Bob Yates' extra point was good and Syracuse led 7–6 in the waning seconds of the first quarter.

Starting the second quarter at their own 20-yard line, Holy Cross had a minus two yards on three attempts and again was forced to punt. Joern, under a heavy rush, this time got off a beautiful, high spiral that a backpedaling Ernie Davis caught at the Syracuse 34. Sidestepping two defenders, Davis picked up a block along the sideline and returned the ball 15 yards before being knocked out of bounds near midfield. Syracuse, on three running plays, advanced the ball seven yards to the Holy Cross 44. On fourth and three, Syracuse decided to go for it. Interestingly, Schwartzwalder had added a trick play in practice that week.

MAURY YOUMANS (Tackle): "Ben had put in a trick play off our punt formation for the Holy Cross game. Ben's punt formation al-

Syracuse picks up some tough yards. Courtesy of Gerhard Schwedes.

ways had two lineman and the quarterback setup in the backfield in front of the punter, Tom Gilburg. This play called for Gilburg to throw a short screen-pass to the outside lineman or the quarterback. Since Bob Yates was set up as the outside lineman, either he or the quarterback would be the receiver. I was ticked off. I thought I should be the outside lineman. Hell, I was an end my first two years at Syracuse and Bob had always played tackle. I thought I would be the better receiver. I didn't dare say anything about it to Ben. Well, when they called the play in the game, Gilburg says, 'I don't think I can throw it.' Gerhard says, 'Okay, I'll throw it.' Yates then says, 'I don't think I can catch it.' I immediately said 'I'll catch it,' and that's when I had my moment of glory. I caught the pass and ran 10 yards for a first down. Schwedes told me later he wanted to throw the pass to Sarette, but he was covered, so he was forced to throw it to me."

Syracuse took advantage of the first down, and behind the powerful running of Baker and Schwedes, moved to the Holy Cross 4. Schwartzwalder, for the third time in the game, was faced with a tough fourth down decision. Deciding against a sure three points, Ben called for a play-action pass. Sarette, after the fake handoff, dropped back and lofted a pass to the corner of the end zone to an open Ernie Davis. Closing fast, the Crusader's Dick Skinner was able at the last second to tip the ball away. Holy Cross had held again! Taking over, the Crusaders were unable to move the ball and again forced to punt. Syracuse's John Brown collided with the Holy Cross backup punter John Bocklet in the end zone. Roughing the kicker was called on Brown and Holy Cross had a gift first down. The Crusaders were still unable to move the ball against Syracuse's second unit and had to kick it away. Booklet, once again hurried by Brown, hit a short, line-drive punt which Reimer returned to the Holy Cross 34-yard line. The second unit, staying on the field, gained two yards on two running plays bringing up a third and eight. Second team quarterback Dick Easterly, having called for an option-pass, rolled to the weakside of the field, saw an opening and ran to the Crusader 10 before Purmuto knocked him out of bounds. On first down, Easterly dropped back to pass and hooked up with lanky Tom Gilburg for a touchdown. Gilburg, running a crossing pattern, caught the ball at the 5-yard line and bulled his way into the end zone. Backup kicker Al Gerlick added the extra point and Syracuse led 14–6.

Holy Cross, now trailing by eight points, decided to pass. Starting quarterback Joern, under a heavy rush, threw wildly upfield, with the pass being intercepted by Reimer at the Holy Cross 40-yard line. Reimer, coming up from his safety position, made a diving catch on the errant throw. On first down Syracuse ran their famous "scissors play" with Ernie Davis bursting through the weak side of the Crusader defense. Shoulder-faking one defender, Number 44 turned the corner at midfield and jetted by three defenders for the touchdown. Gerlick's kick was wide but Syracuse now led 20–6.

Doctor/coach Anderson, realizing this game was getting away from him, decided to change quarterbacks and replaced Joern with Junior Dick Komodzinski. Seeing his first action at quarterback, Komodzinski promptly hit right end Charlie Pacunas deep across the middle. Wrestling the ball away from Syracuse defender Schwedes, Pacunas gained 38 yards on the play giving Holy Cross a first down at the Syracuse's 39-yard line. With the rain beginning to fall, Komodzinski went to the air again and tried to force a pass between two Orange defenders. Schwedes, not to be outdone again, intercepted the ball at the Syracuse 34. Syracuse had the ball back with less than a minute to go in the half.

Easterly, staying in the game at quarterback with the first unit, found Schwedes on a crossing route for 27 yards and a first down at the Holy Cross 39. With only twenty-five seconds to go, Easterly went back to Schwedes, who caught the ball on the far sideline and jumped out-of-bounds at the Holy Cross 19 stopping the clock. There were eleven seconds left in the half.

Easterly, dropping back to pass, was forced out of the pocket by Promuto. Dodging and rolling to his right, Easterly looked for Ernie Davis across the middle. Finding him covered and feeling the Crusader defense closing in on him, Easterly reversed field, desperately looking to find somebody open. Avoiding one defender, Easterly, as he approached the line of scrimmage, spotted Schwedes breaking free at the 5-yard line. With the game clock showing zeros, Easterly hit Schwedes with a perfect pass as the captain fell into the end zone for the touchdown. The stadium went crazy. The local kid had put on a dazzling display of passing and the Orange led a stunned Holy Cross team 26–6. Schwartzwalder decided to go for two. Easterly, brimming with confidence, found Skonieczski open for the two-point conversion. At the halfway mark, Syracuse had extended its lead to 28–6.

The Orangemen took the second half kickoff and showed they were not about to let up. Moving the ball quickly to the Holy Cross 34 yard-line, Sarette found Skonieczski open down the middle. Skonieczski caught the pass at the 3-yard line and walked into the end zone untouched. Yates kick made it 35–6.

The game's last touchdown came in the fourth period when Schwedes, taking the ball at the Holy Cross 9-yard line, burst off left tackle for the touchdown. Yates' extra point made it 42–6.

Captain Gerhard Schwedes had led the way against Holy Cross. The senior halfback had gained 97 yards on 13 carries and scored a touchdown. He had five catches in the game for 82 yards and another score. He also completed one pass for 10 yards and on defense intercepted one. He was chosen Most Valuable Player in the game, and received the Frazier Memorial Trophy for his exploits.

Syracuse, in winning its fourth straight game, had defeated an overmatched Holy Cross team. Schwartzwalder, playing his two talented teams equally (thirty-nine players in all), just wore down the undermanned Crusaders. Holy Cross had a minus 28 yards rushing, due in a large part to the total domination at the line of scrimmage by Syracuse's two outstanding lines. Holy Cross quarterbacks, scrambling for their lives, were intercepted five times. The game was so one-sided that after Holy Cross scored in the first period, they could cross midfield only once more the remainder of the game. Syracuse signal-callers passed for four touchdowns, two each by Sarette and Easterly. Syracuse completed 13 of 27 passes for 208 yards. The Orange gained 257 yards on the ground, picking up 22 first downs.

EDDIE ANDERSON (Holy Cross Head Coach): "This was the best Syracuse team I've ever faced. We hoped to give them a better game, but they are a really strong outfit. They are very explosive. They have good running, good passing, and a fine defense. When they can get their backs past the line there's a good chance they will go all the way. If you can think of anything to add, say it in the superlative."

VINCE PROMUTO (Holy Cross Lineman): "We had them stopped cold early in the game but they were too good. They just didn't have any fear and nothing scared them. They would just come back at you and move you out of the way. That's a real solid team."

MARK WEBER (Halfback): "A friend of mine, who went to Holy Cross at that time, tells a story about our '59 team playing them. He says when we came out on the field before the game we looked like the Huns. They were big, they were mean, and there were a lot of them. Holy Cross had a good first team but after that they were thin. Syracuse just kept sending in fresh troops. The second half Holy Cross was just beat up, they couldn't handle it."

DICK EASTERLY (Quarterback): "Everybody knew who Vince Promuto was. He was kind of an ugly looking guy who looked like Jack Palance. I come down on a kickoff and I designated myself to whack him and let me just say that he reversed it, he whacked me down good. He lifted me right in the air and that's something I remember vividly about that play. But we won the game."

Ben Schwartzwalder was pleased with the win but concerned about injuries to reserve backs Reimer and Anderson. Reimer separated his shoulder in the second half and would be out three games. Anderson badly sprained his ankle in the fourth quarter and was carried off the field. He was also projected to miss up to three games. Both players had been key contributors for Syracuse in the first part of the season and would be sorely missed.

BEN SCHWARTZWALDER: "I'd rather take back four touchdowns than lose those kids."

Syracuse, now 4–0 and certain to move up in the polls, had West Virginia coming to Archbold Stadium next week. The year before Syracuse had escaped with their lives in Morgantown, winning 15–12. The players were looking forward to the contest but were well aware, as the media and Syracuse fans were, that Penn State was looming in the background.

Roger Davis. Courtesy of Syracuse University Sports information.

11

"Hound Dog, the Dingleman and Friends..."

Roger Davis was raised in Solon, Ohio, the son of a tavern keeper. Besides playing sports, Roger liked to play cards and train 'coon' dogs which is why he was nicknamed 'Hound dog,' at Syracuse. A great athlete, he was absolutely fearless in his approach to life and always went at his own pace. Davis, who was well-liked and respected by his teammates, was friendly with everybody. Fiercely loyal to his friends, it was always an interesting night when you went out with him. When you got into Roger's car, there was no telling where you were going to end up.

PAT WHELAN (End): "Roger and I were out, and when we were coming back, it was snowing hard. I took a turn too sharp and slid and hit the wagon of the 'Dingleman,' the guy who drove around, rang the bell, and sold hamburgers to the students. Roger went up against the dash board and cut himself up real bad. He wasn't going to go for help. Finally they came and towed the car away so Roger and I walked down to the clinic which was open 24 hours. We get in there and they put Roger on the table, and I said to Roger, 'We got to leave, the cops are coming.' The doctor says, 'You can't leave,' and I said, 'Well watch me.' He says, 'I'm not through sewing him up.' I said, 'Sew him up, we're getting out of here.' I'm trying to pick Roger up off the table and the doctor pushes me away and he calls for the Head Nurse as I'm trying to get Roger out of there. Finally the doctor says, 'If you'll calm down, I'll get him sewn up in less than a minute, and you guys can leave. I want you out of here.' We got thrown out of the clinic. Later someone says to Roger, 'Why don't you sue Whelan?' Roger says, 'Hey, that sounds like a good deal.' So Roger sued me. I flipped it over to the insurance company, the insurance company eventually paid Roger. Roger called me and said, 'I got the money, let's go!' We went out on a toot, and had a hell of a time."

DICK BEYER (Assistant Coach): "Let me tell you a story about Roger Davis. He comes in his freshmen year and all the coaches come up to me and say, 'How's the kid doing?' I'm the frosh line coach. They wanted to know if this kid was as good as they thought he was. See, Roger Davis was a kid Bill Bell recruited down in Ohio. I come in and I make the statement, I says, 'If that Roger Davis is a football player, I'm a monkey's uncle.' Well, Jesus Christ, now they jump me. I says, 'Christ, he can't even hit the sleds, he couldn't hit the blocking dummy.' Later on I found out they didn't have them in his school. A few years later, when he's voted the top lineman in the country, winning the Outland Trophy (Awarded to the best college lineman), an unanimous All-America selection, I said, 'You're looking at a monkey's uncle.' He became a great defensive player, especially his freshmen year. We would put him on the weak side and he would knife in; he was quick. I think the Chicago Bears missed their calling when they drafted him and put him at offensive guard. He should have been on defense. He would have made a great defensive lineman in the pro's."

MAURY YOUMANS (Tackle): "I think Roger was a bit misplaced in pro ball. Roger could play both offense and defense great. I think he was a better defensive ballplayer than an offensive ballplayer. When you get drafted in the pros, they normally draft you for a position that they need. It might be they are going to lose somebody to retirement, or injury. Many times they are weak at that position or need to add depth. The Bears needed a guard and so they took Roger as a guard. He was fast and quick. Before the play he wouldn't move very fast. You could light a fire under his ass and he would move slowly. But as soon as the play started, he was off and running. He was very strong, but he was very quick. I remember him playing against the Colt's Gene "Big Daddy" Lipscomb. He hardly had a mark on him. Then he played against Alex Karras with Detroit. He came out of that game all cut up. His face was bruised. Alex used to come right up into you, with a forearm. Big Daddy would softly walk the line. He was more a pursuer. But Roger handled both of them fairly well."

DAVE APPELHOF (Center): "Roger and I were roommates in '59. One thing I can say about Roger, he had the messiest room you would ever see. Dirty clothes everywhere. When he was getting ready to go to New York, to receive the Outland Trophy, for 'Best Lineman,' he scrambled around to find something clean to wear. A few weeks later I looked over to his part of the room and there's the Outland Trophy in the corner, covered with dirty clothes."

DICK EASTERLY (Quarterback): "Roger Davis was a unique type of guy. We all considered him the unsung captain of that team. He was one of the key leaders, leading without trying to lead. Roger was just a great ball player all the way around, both offense and defense."

ROGER DAVIS (Guard): "One time a bunch of the guys on the team went to that Italian joint Nappy's. I had been at a wedding with the people I knew from Syracuse that trained dogs. When I get there, I see there's a seat at the bar next to Jim Saylor. Saylor was feeling no pain and was talking to this guy's girl. I hear Saylor say to this girl, 'Your eyes are like pools.' Usually you're going to follow it up with something beautiful. Instead Saylor says, 'Your eyes are like pools . . . Cesspools.' Well, that started the fight. I actually went to break it up because I hadn't been out with them all day and I wasn't in bad shape. Well, this guy smacked me a couple of times and I just took a roundhouse and he just walked right into it. That was the end of him. I broke his jaw and they took him to the hospital. The guy said later that I hit him with an ashtray but I didn't. As it turns out, this guy was a professional fighter. He was a good friend of the heavyweight boxer from back then, Mike DeJohn. DeJohn's brother was in the bar. Now he was mad and almost got into it with poor Al Gerlick."

JP BYRNES (Friend of the Team): "I remember the time Roger

Jim Saylor. Courtesy of Pat Whelan.

Pat Whelan and Roger Davis planning a night out! Courtesy of Pat Whelan.

was coming back from Colgate. He was down there playing poker. He had driven into a snowbank on the way back and had no way to get the car out, so he left it. He called somebody up to come get him and just left the car. I remember, like a week later, we went down there to get the car out. We went down there and the car is plowed in. It took us a long while just to find it. Today the car would have probably been long gone after a couple of days, but back then, it was still there. Roger wasn't the least worried about that car."

MAURY YOUMANS (Tackle): "Roger and I were both drafted by the Chicago Bears. We used to room together with the Bears. Roger had a propensity for walking in his sleep. We were scheduled to play an exhibition game in Norfolk, Virginia. It was funny because we were playing in the same stadium where we played Navy, the Oyster Bowl. We were down there playing the Redskins in a Saturday night game. It's Friday night, I'm watching television, and he falls asleep. So I turn the lights out. We got twin beds and I go to blow my nose. He must have heard me blow my nose. He got up out of his bed, growls and he grabbed me by the throat. He and I and the mattress all went off on the floor. Now it's dead quiet in that room and I'm scared to death. I'm hitting him on the shoulder, "Roger, Roger, Roger." And he finally woke up. Well needless to say, I had a chair in between Roger and me whenever we roomed together after that. He said later that he was dreaming that there was a masked man in the room. How that had any effect on his sleep walking, I don't know, but I always had that chair between us after that."

BOB STEM (Center): "I remember Dave Baker used to sing the song 'Old Shep' to Roger, and Roger would cry. It used to make him tear up."

Jerry Skonieczki gets behind the Mountaineer Defense. Courtesy of Syracuse University Archives.

12

West Virginia

Every year leading into 1959 the Syracuse football games against West Virginia had been hard fought. The series between the two schools began in 1945 with the Orange winning the inaugural game at home, 12–0. In 1946 Syracuse traveled to Morgantown to face the Mountaineers. Syracuse's head coach, Clarence "Biggie" Munn, decided to house his players thirty miles outside of Morgantown in Summit, Pennsylvania. Munn, in his only year of coaching football at Syracuse, felt it would be quieter in Summit and hoped it would help the players prepare better for the upcoming game. He also thought the scenic trip on Saturday morning through the mountains would be a serene and quiet trip as well as a good environment for the players on game day.

Munn, who was big on mental preparation, liked his practices and his pre-game schedules to be precise. The former All-America football player at Minnesota always posted a sign in his locker rooms that said; "The difference between good and great is a little extra effort." Well, when this game was done, Biggie probably figured the good folks at West Virginia had put in that little extra effort to help his team lose. According to Biggie, this effort included hiring a crazy bus driver to "scare the hell," out of his players on their drive to Morgantown. Driving the curvy mountain roads at breakneck speeds, Munn, finally exasperated, demanded the driver stop the bus. Taking the driver outside, Munn, with his finger in the frightened man's chest, screamed. "We can't play this football game, if we crack up here on this mountain road you crazy son of a bitch. You're scaring the hell out of my players and you're scaring me. Now, I don't give a damn if you were paid to do that or not, you're going to slow this bus down so we can enjoy this ride. I don't care if we're late for the game, you're going to slow this bus down. NOW! Or we're throwing you out and I'll drive the damn bus to the game." The driver slowed down but the die was cast and Syracuse was beaten that day, 13–0. After the game, Munn was furious about the loss and always complained bitterly that the bus driver contributed to his team's poor effort.

Biggie left Syracuse for Michigan State after the 1946 season, finishing his only year on the hill at 4–5. Moving on to Michigan State, he posted a 52–9–0 record in seven seasons as head coach. His 1952 team went 9–0 and was the consensus number one team in the nation, and Munn was named coach of the year. Following the 1953 season he became athletic director and turned the coaching reigns over to another former Syracuse coach, Forrest "Duffy" Daugherty.

In 1955 Syracuse renewed its rivalry with West Virginia, and the Mountaineers would now become a constant on the Syracuse football schedule. Each year since Ben Schwartzwalder arrived in 1949, the schedule improved in its quality of competitive opponents. Weak sisters such as Fordham, Villanova, and Niagra were no longer a part of the Syracuse football schedule. Teams like Cornell and Colgate still remained on the schedule in the late fifties, but it was apparent their days were numbered in being able to compete against the bigger Eastern schools like Syracuse.

Syracuse had won three of the four games played in the renewed series with West Virginia, winning in 1955 and 1956 before losing in 1957, 7–0. West Virginia had thoroughly outplayed the Orangemen in Morgantown in last year's contest but lost where it counts most, on the scoreboard, 15–12. Each battle in the fifties had been close, and most sportswriters thought this year's game would again be competitive.

West Virginia's head coach, Art "Pappy" Lewis, had been at the helm of the Mountaineers since 1950. He grew up in Mason County, West Virginia, the same area that Ben Schwartzwalder had grown up in. Lewis, an All-American tackle at Ohio University in the mid-1930s, was renown for developing lineman, and his interior players were always very good. His '59 team was no exception.

Led by Bill "Hardcoal" Lopasky, a 6'1', 225-pound guard, the Mountaineers presented perhaps the most physical line Syracuse would face this season. Lopasky, the son of a Pennsylvania coal miner, had developed his rock-hard physique digging graves with his father who doubled as a cemetery caretaker. In last week's upset win over Pittsburgh, Lopasky actually stole the ball out of Pitt's quarterback Ivan Tonsic's hand as he was getting ready to pass. Beating the Panthers 23–15, West Virginia came into the Syracuse game with a 3–2 record.

Pappy Lewis, who at the beginning of the season thought that his team would start slowly because of inexperience, had his squad beginning to play well. Quarterback Danny Williams was a strong runner who was also a capable passer. A highly recruited player his senior year in high school, the tobacco chewing field general was developing into a first rate quarterback. Operating out of a straight-T offense, the Mountaineer backfield also included two speedy halfbacks. Left halfback Ray Peterson was the reigning Southern Conference sprint champion, having been clocked at 9.8 seconds in the hundred-yard dash. Starting right halfback John Marra was a fine all-around player who was currently ranked seventh in the nation in receiving. Fullbacks Bob Benke and Tom Hudson provided West Virginia with two physical players to complement the speed of Williams, Peterson and Marra. Syracuse scout Bill Bell had some well founded concerns about West Virginia.

BILL BELL (Assistant Coach): "They have as fine a backfield as we'll see all year. With their speed, we will probably see a lot of traffic around our ends. Also that front line is very good. They sure get after the quarterback."

The week prior to Pittsburgh playing West Virginia, Pitt scout Steve Petro had issued a stern warning to the highly favored Pitt team. "This West Virginia is a much better team than their record indicates. They are the most aggressive team you will ever see. Their line is big and strong, and they have great speed in the backfield. They can give anybody a game." Pitt, a thirteen-point favorite, didn't listen and got soundly beaten.

The Syracuse head coach wasn't taking this game for granted and worked his team hard during the week, with emphasis on stopping the Mountaineers' outside running game.

BEN SCHWARTZWALDER: "They'll try to go to the outside, just like last year, so we might as well be ready."

Compounding the preparation for West Virginia was the injuries suffered by running backs Jim Anderson and Whitey Reimer last week against Holy Cross. Schwartzwalder decided to move junior John Nichols up from the third group to replace the injured Anderson. Nichols, from nearby Cortland, had been given little opportunity to carry the ball so far this season. A very aggressive linebacker on defense, he had scored one rushing touchdown in Syracuse's second game of the year against Maryland. Nichols for the season had 36 yards on 8 carries. Replacing Reimer proved to be a bit more difficult. Reimer had been a terrific two-way player for Schwartzwalder this season. Lately Ben had been experimenting playing Reimer with the first team on defense much of the last two games. The junior running back, though only 5'9" and 158 pounds, was a small but fearless player, just as his head coach had been twenty-five years earlier.

BEN SCHWARTZWALDER: "The loss of Reimer has set off a chain reaction. The easiest thing would be to move someone up a notch, from the third string, but it isn't that simple with regards to Whitey. Were already too thin at halfback, so we will have to juggle around."

First, Schwartzwalder decided to move 5'10", 175-pound halfback Bobby Hart to the second team on offense. Hart, from Bellevue, Ohio, had good speed and was very good in the open field. If the second group was substituted in on defense, senior Ed Bowers would get the call. Bowers, who already had two interceptions for the year, was a 6', 175-pounder from Tonawanda, New York. Bowers was a tough guy who played with an attitude. He wouldn't back down from anything and Schwartzwalder knew he would get a good effort from Bowers.

As the game approached, the West Virginia head coach was very

Tom Gilburg gives West Virgina the evil eye. Courtesy of Syracuse University Archives.

complimentary of the Orangemen and went to great lengths to extol their virtues.

PAPPY LEWIS (West Virginia Head Coach): "Our scouts report you have one of the finest teams in the country. You're a lot bigger and you have tremendous bench strength. We don't have the depth, neither do we have size."

When Schwartzwalder heard that Lewis told the press West Virginia didn't have size, he went through the roof.

BEN SCHWARTZWALDER: "In all my years here at Syracuse we've never fielded a team as big as any West Virginia team. This team is no exception. They'll have 35 to 40 of the biggest, healthiest boys you have ever seen. They could be hungrier than we are. I hope the Pitt game will shock our players. This is not the week to relax."

Syracuse had moved up in the polls to number six. Defending champion LSU was still undefeated and ranked number one, followed in the polls by Northwestern, Texas, Mississippi, and Southern California. All the teams above Syracuse were undefeated. The Orange were number one in the nation in total defense and scoring. They remained marginally ahead of Penn State in the Lambert Trophy race followed by Army and Pittsburgh. The Nittany Lions, at 5–0, cracked the Top

Ten in the national polls for the first time, moving up to number eight. Yale, undefeated and unscored upon through five games, moved into the top twenty at number nineteen.

Thirty-five thousand fans showed up at rain-spattered Archbold Stadium on October 24, 1959, to watch Syracuse take on West Virginia. The 'Parents' Weekend' crowd cheered as the undefeated, sixth-ranked Orangemen took the field. West Virginia, after winning the toss, returned the kickoff to their own 24-yard line. Mountaineer quarterback Danny Williams, on first down, ran around left end for 10 yards and a first down. On second down halfback John Marra burst off-tackle for another 10 yards. West Virginia's burly line early on was having the best of it. The Mountaineers, quickly coming to the line on first down, set up in their straight "T-formation." Williams, attempting to run wide to the right, was hit for a 5-yard loss by Syracuse defenders Bruce Tarbox and Ed Bowers. On second and fifteen, Williams attempted to pass, but was sacked by Roger Davis for a 6-yard loss. Facing third and 21, the Mountaineers ran a draw play netting 4 yards and the visitors were forced to punt.

Syracuse, following the punt, went to work on the ground beginning at their own 27. Mark Weber, off tackle, gained 10 yards. Dave Sarette then came back to Weber on a short pass for another 10-yard gain. After Gerhard Schwedes gained 3 yards off-tackle, Sarette hit Ernie Davis with a short completion. The Elmira native in turn pitched the ball to Art Baker who motored past midfield down to the West Virginia 40. The Orange, now with a first down in West Virginia territory, went back to Art Baker. Two carries by the Syracuse fullback moved the ball to the Mountaineer 27. Schwartzwalder, seeing West Virginia couldn't stop Baker, called a third straight play for him. Running straight up the middle, Baker sprinted 23 yards before being dragged down at the Mountaineer 4. Staying on the ground, Schwedes scored the game's first touchdown. Bob Yates's kick gave Syracuse the early lead, 7–0.

West Virginia, after those initial first downs, could not move the ball on two successive possessions. As the second quarter began Syracuse had the ball at their own 22-yard line. Sarette, dropping back to pass, spotted end Jerry Skonieczki wide open at the 40. Skonieczki, catching Sarette's pass, broke open on a huge block from Ernie Davis and sprinted down to the West Virginia 20-yard line. Going back to the ground game, Schwedes sprinted around left end for 12 yards before being knocked out-of-bounds at the 8-yard line. West Virginia was also assessed with a penalty when Schwedes was punched after the whistle by Mountaineer linemen Glenn Bowman. Schwedes, getting some revenge, dove in the end zone for the touchdown. Yates's kick made it 14–0.

West Virginia's offensive woes continued as two consecutive running plays netted only 2 yards. Williams, being rushed hard by the Syracuse front four, threw an errant pass that was caught by an ineligible receiver, that same Glenn Bowman. The Mountaineers were forced to punt. Dave Sarette grabbed Williams' punt at his own 21 and sidestepped up the sidelines for 22 yards. On first down at their 43, Syracuse ran the "scissors play" for Ernie Davis. The fleet sophomore running back burst through the line untouched, darted to the outside, and set sail for the goal line. Having one man to beat, Mountaineer defender Dave Rider, Davis just flew by him on a 57-yard jaunt for the touchdown. The Elmira Express had arrived! West Virginia blocked Yates' third extra point try but still trailed 20–0.

The Mountaineers were now being crushed by the Syracuse defense. Unable to move the ball at all, Danny Williams was forced to punt again. Second unit leader Al Gerlick, busting through, partially blocked Williams' punt, again giving Syracuse great field position. The Orange moved the chains but a series of penalties stalled the drive. Bob Yates came on to kick a 35-yard field goal to stretch the lead to 23–0. The Mountaineers, still unable to move the ball, were forced to punt again. Syracuse's second unit moved down the field as reserve fullback Gary Fallon, on his first carry of the season, rambled 20 yards for a first down. Quarterback Dick Easterly's 21-yard pass completion to Tom Gilburg moved the ball to the West Virginia 23 with 15 seconds to go in the half. Syracuse, on first down, ran a halfback-pass with Mark Weber finding Ken Erickson deep in the back of the end zone for the score. Yates converted the extra point as the half ended, extending the Syracuse lead to 30–0.

West Virginia players and coaches walked off the field totally demoralized. No one expected West Virginia to be trailing by thirty points at halftime. The Mountaineers, even though losing last year, kicked Syracuse all over the field. Pappy Lewis watched his team in the first half being totally outclassed.

West Virginia did come out in the second half and play better defensively, holding the Orange at bay early on. Offensive was another story as they continued to struggle. Williams, playing almost entirely at quarterback, completed a few passes but not enough to put a sustained drive together.

Syracuse, late in the third quarter, started a drive from their own 20-yard line. Moving on the ground behind the strong running of Ernie Davis, Syracuse scored again off the scissors play, this time from the West Virginia 29. Although other players ran the scissors for Syracuse over the years, no one had the talent to run this misdirection play like Davis.

Syracuse finished the scoring for the game at the beginning of the fourth period. After receiving the ball at midfield, the Orange, behind the running of Mark Weber and John Nichols, pushed the ball to the 2-yard line. Weber scored over right guard and Gerlick's kick made it 44–0. The Mountaineers did move the ball against the Syracuse reserves but never did score, and the game came to a merciful ending.

Pappy Lewis, always a delight for reporters, had nothing to say following the game. He refused to meet with the press and released no statement. Perhaps the Mountaineer head coach thought his counterpart rubbed it in a bit, but we will never know, as Lewis never said anything about the game. His halftime talk to his team did give some idea of his feelings.

ARNIE BURDICK (Sports Editor, *Herald Journal,* 1959): "It was halftime and the visiting dressing room was unusually quiet as trainer Whitey Gwynn attended to a bunch of minor hurts. Finally it was time for the second half and head coach Pappy Lewis, down 30–0, addressed his troops this way. 'Boys, I just don't know what to tell you. . . . so just protect yourselves the best way you know how.' That was his halftime speech."

BEN SCHWARTZWALDER: "I felt a little sorry for Pappy. You don't try to roll up a score, but when your kids play well in there, it happens. I don't think West Virginia was up for this game like they were for Pittsburgh. Our team could have gone all the way against anybody today."

High praise from Ben who was surprised at how strong his team played. It didn't matter which group he put in the game, they all played well. Ben made a point of praising the third team for their play, mentioning Norm Lemeuix and Pete Brokaw. Ernie Davis started to show glimpses of his greatness, gaining 141 yards on just 9 carries. Weber, alternating with Davis, gained 72 yards, and was 2 of 2 in passing for 30 yards and a touchdown.

MARK WEBER (Halfback): "I remember the West Virginia game. I had a great game but it was overshadowed by Ernie's performance. The first two plays of the game from scrimmage were designed for Ernie but he broke his shoulder pad laces on the kickoff and I was sent in to run those plays. The first play was off-tackle and I gained 10 yards. The next play I think was a short pass to me that gained another 10 yards. So Ernie gets his pads fixed and he comes back in for me. I'm thinking to myself, what did I do wrong?"

Syracuse dominated the statistics as expected. The Orange had 27 first downs to the visitors' 7. Syracuse amassed 455 yards on the ground and 134 yards through the air. The defense held West Virginia to a total of 109 yards for the game. The Mountaineers gained 60 yards on the ground and another 49 yards through the air, completing just 5 passes out of 21 attempts.

Syracuse came through the game unscathed and with five wins in the bank. They now could get ready to go to Pittsburgh and face the up-and-down Panthers. Schwartzwalder knew one thing for sure: Pittsburgh wouldn't take his Orangemen lightly. He only hoped that he could get the same effort from his team next week.

Jerry Skonieczki makes a diving catch against Pittsburgh.
Courtesy of Pat Whelan.

13

Pittsburgh

The Syracuse Juggernaut," is how one fan described the Orangemen through the first half of the '59 season. Syracuse, after its impressive win over West Virginia, moved up to number five in the AP poll, switching spots with Southern California who struggled to beat Stanford. LSU remained number one for the thirteenth week in a row, followed by Northwestern, Mississippi, and Texas. Penn State, still undefeated, was number seven in the weekly polls. Syracuse, for the first time all season, had garnered 11 first place votes and was starting to get some respect around the country. The national magazines, Sports Illustrated and The Sporting News, featured articles on the powerful Orangemen, and the added attention would do nothing but help the team's national image.

VAL PINCHBACK (Syracuse Sports Information Director, 1959): "I used to go down to New York every Monday to the writers' luncheon. Occasionally I'd take Benny down but not every week. I'd go over to the Associated Press and they basically counted all the votes for the weekly poll. In those days everybody subscribing to the AP service got to vote. Lo and behold, we found out that little radio stations in Mississippi, or Florida, or Texas, somewhere down there, would vote for the Southern teams and they'd leave out Syracuse, they'd leave out

Southern Cal. In other words, those teams didn't get any additional votes, they didn't get ANY votes. So eventually they made an internal decision that if somebody voting didn't at least cast a vote for the three major unbeaten teams in the top ten, they threw out the vote. That helped us in the polls as the season went on. The guys up North wouldn't do it, in other words nobody in Syracuse, or in Ithaca, or in Rome would send in votes for Syracuse and leave out Southern teams."

Syracuse, moving up to number five, attained the highest ranking (up to that point) of any Syracuse football team in the school's history. The '56 team, led by Jim Brown, reached as high as number six, and last year's team reached number nine. The Orange continued to dominate the statistics: First in the country in total offense, first in scoring(36.4), and first in total defense. Number three ranked Mississippi was second in total defense, followed by number one ranked LSU. Those two Southern teams would square off Saturday night in Baton Rouge, so the Orangemen knew the opportunity to fly higher in the polls probably would be there with an impressive win over Pittsburgh.

The up-and-down Panthers (3–3) would field on Saturday approximately the same team that had lost last year's game in Archbold Stadium, 16–13. Losing only their two guards and a halfback from the '58 team, Pittsburgh was expected to challenge Syracuse and Penn State for the Lambert Trophy. Their season had been disappointing thus far. After impressive wins over Marquette, Duke, and UCLA, the Panthers lost their next two games, being upset two weeks ago by West Virginia, then losing last week to 15th ranked TCU.

Pittsburgh was led by senior quarterback Ivan 'The Terrible' Tonsic and junior end Mike Ditka. Tonsic, after throwing four touchdowns against UCLA, had been flat the past two weeks and had played poorly. The 5'11", 185-pound quarterback for the season had thrown for 563 yards and 7 touchdowns. Unfortunately, he had been intercepted 13 times. Pittsburgh's head coach, John Michelson, understood that against Syracuse and their powerful front lines his lineman had better be able to give Tonsic some time to throw or it could be a long afternoon for his team. Also, on the other side of the ball, Syracuse's number one rated offense had many weapons from which to attack.

DARRELL LEWIS (Pittsburgh Scout,1959): "I remember when I was playing (Pitt Quarterback, '55,'56) the only thing you had to do was defense Jimmy Brown. We seemed to have pretty good luck doing that because we beat them two years running. Now this present Orange team is a real fine team. They're by far the best Orange team that I have ever seen. They have so many threats that you don't know where to begin to stop them. You can't load up on one man like we did with Brown because another guy will murder you."

JOHN MICHELSON (Pittsburgh Head Coach): "Syracuse has good size and depth, and in Ernie Davis and Art Baker, they have two of the finest backs in the country. But don't forget about Gerhard Schwedes. He's their bread and butter man. He gets the tough yards for them when they need them."

Ernie Davis was coming off his best game of his young college career gaining 141 yards on just 9 carries against West Virginia. This averaged out to 15.6 yards per carry which broke Jim Brown's Syracuse single-game record of 12.9 yards per carry, set during the 1955 season. When asked about bettering a Brown record the modest Davis said, " I'll never beat him, he's the best." 'Number 44' was getting comfortable in the Syracuse offense. "I'm getting the feel of it," is the way he described it to the press. The young sophomore back had gained 371 yards on 49 carries, he had caught 7 passes for 60 yards, and he had scored 4 touchdowns. Davis was coming on strong and so were his teammates.

Coach Schwartzwalder was not comfortable with all the high praise his team was receiving. Pittsburgh was always a formidable opponent, and the last 2 games against the Panthers had been decided by 3 points. Ben was worried that with Penn State coming up next week and his team's blowout of West Virginia last week, his team's concentration would not be there. He worried that all the national recognition and his team's ascension in the polls would go to the players' heads.

BEN SCHWARTZWALDER: "If Pitt puts together a first quarter like they did against Duke or a fourth quarter like they did against UCLA, they'll run us right off the field. We were just plain lucky to beat Kansas, Maryland, Navy, Holy Cross, and West Virginia. If we played some of those games over we wouldn't do as well."

Nobody believed old Ben but he needed to make sure his boys were ready for Pittsburgh.

The city of Pittsburgh was in the midst of a steel workers' strike as the Panthers prepared to host Syracuse on Homecoming Day, October 30, 1959. The strike, now entering its 107th day, was effecting everything in the Steel City, including attendance at Panther home games. A crowd of only 25,000 was expected for the 15th renewal of this outstanding series.

Syracuse, under rainy, dreary skies, kicked off to begin the game. Playing again without top reserves Whitey Reimer and Jim Anderson, the Orange quickly put to rest any notion that they were looking ahead to Penn State. Stopping Pittsburgh on three straight plays, Syracuse, following a poor punt by Mike Ditka, started from Pittsburgh's 37-yard line. Five plays later the Orange scored, the touchdown set up by a 30-yard pass from Dave Sarette to Jerry Skonieczki. Gerhard Schwedes scored from the 1 and Bob Yates provided the extra point.

Early in the second quarter, still leading 7–0, Syracuse drove to the Pittsburgh 25. Ernie Davis, off the "scissors play," galloped 25 yards for the touchdown. The power of the Syracuse offensive front wall operating out of the unbalanced line right was forcing opponent defenses to move more men up to the right side of the line of scrimmage. Upon seeing this, Syracuse would come back with the "scissors play." This misdirection back to the left allowed Davis to showcase his God-given abilities. Running to the weak side against the defensive flow, Davis would pick his opening and then just outrun the defenders. His blend of power and speed made this play almost impossible to contain.

Syracuse owned the line of scrimmage throughout the game. Schwartzwalder, alternating his two powerful lines, reeked havoc on the Panthers. Dozens of times the Syracuse defensive lineman would break through the line throwing Pitt running backs for losses.

Syracuse would score again in the third period, this time on a nifty 23-yard run by fullback Art Baker. Baker, after receiving a lateral from

Davis, ran untouched into the end zone, high-stepping the last 10 yards to draw the ire of frustrated Pittsburgh defender Mike Ditka.

The Syracuse offense scored once more in the fourth quarter as the second unit marched 70 yards before Mark Weber jammed it in from 1 yard out. Al Gerlick added the extra point.

Leading 28–0, Schwartzwalder emptied the bench and gave the reserves an opportunity to play. Pittsburgh, now moving the ball against Syracuse backups had a first down deep in Syracuse territory at the Orange 9-yard line. Dropping back to pass in the waning moments of the game, Pitt's backup quarterback threw toward the end zone. Syracuse linebacker Dan Rackiewicz, one yard deep in the end zone, stepped in front of the Pittsburgh receiver and intercepted the pass. Rackiewicz, who had made the trip to Pittsburgh because of the injury to Anderson, then began his journey toward the Pittsburgh goal line and a place in Syracuse football history.

DAN RACKIEWICZ (Linebacker): "Needless to say I was a scrub. I was a third stringer that game. It was toward the end of the game sometime in the fourth quarter and Pittsburgh was just passing like crazy going down the field. I was chided for my slowness but I'm here to tell you, I thought I was a linebacker. We were on pass defense the whole time, every single play we're covering someone. We were up 28 points. I was just all over the place and I dropped back in my zone and one of their people comes behind me. The quarterback threw the ball right to me, and after a couple of broken field cuts and a lot of dancing and all that, I ran it all the way, 101 yards. I knew it was 101 yards because when I caught it I looked down and I could see I was one yard deep in the end zone."

GERHARD SCHWEDES (Halfback): "When Rackiewicz ran the 101 yards Freddie Mautino was running along side of him . . . sideways. Ron Bartlett and one or two other guys where running along side of him. They would get ahead of him then they would have to slow down and wait for him to catch up. He finally got to score . . . then the comedy of errors really started. Bob Stem was in at center. He was not supposed to center the ball. Pete Brokaw who was not a holder . . . was the holder. George Frankovich was about the fourth string kicker. So they we're all in there at the same time. Stem centered the ball . . . it takes two bounces . . . it hits Brokaw . . . he picks it up off the ground . . . sets it down and it tips over. In the mean time Frankovich is going back and forth trying to kick the ball. So when Pete finally sets it up there was a Pitt lineman dead in front of them. I swear to God, the ball goes under his arms then up and over the goal post."

BEN SCHWARTZWALDER: "It's wonderful when the reserves can stay in there and do something like that. I thought that Pittsburgh was the best team we have faced this season, and we had to play our best in order to lick them. They were hard to defense against. . . . ..rugged. They never quit, they never gave up."

JOHN MICHELSON (Pittsburgh Head Coach): "Syracuse and Southern California are very similar. Syracuse, like USC, is very strong. They kept us in a hole the whole game. The wet field definitely helped them. They were too big for us. That Syracuse line is very good."

Syracuse's Fred Mautino was praised for his outstanding play. The junior end had played magnificently all year, far better than any of the coaches had expected.

BEN SCHWARTZWALDER: "We have never had an end like him, not even Dick Lasse" (former Syracuse player, 1955–57).

Syracuse again dominated the statistics by amassing 387 total yards for the game. Davis led all rushers with 68 yards gained on 10 carries and Art Baker chipped in with 48 yards on 11 attempts. On the other side, quarterback Ivan Tonsic finished the game with a minus 29 yards rushing. Pittsburgh ended up with a net offense of 74 yards, due in large part to the ill-fated drive against the Syracuse reserves near the end of the game.

VAL PINCHBACK (Syracuse Sports Information Director, 1959): "Beano Cook (Pittsburgh Sports Information Director, 1959) insisted that everybody in the press box has to predict a score of the game and put in a dollar. You didn't have to pick the team but just the number of points scored by the two teams. I picked 35. We're ahead 28–0, it's the end of the game, and they're down there about to score, so Beano is running around hollering because I was rooting for Pitt to score so I can get the 35 points. Pittsburgh throws the ball and Rackiewicz picked it off and ran the length of the field, 35 points. I had some smart remark after that. I said, "Beano, I wasn't rooting for Pitt to score, I was just rooting for them to throw an interception and a 100-yard return for the 35 points."

BEANO COOK (Pittsburgh Sports Information Director, 1959): "Everyone had to put a dollar in the pot, or I told them they didn't get stats. I remember there was $43 in the pot—which was a lot of money back then—and Pinchback won it. I always had 17 points. That was a great Syracuse team; they just killed us."

"Another fun night at the Clover Club" (Dick Beyer in one of his many wrestling matches). Courtesy of Dick Beyer.

14

The Clover Club

"I remember when Bob Stem lifted this 220-pound woman up over his shoulders, and did a clean press."
—Dave Appelhof,
Center

"At the Clover Club there were a couple of fights every night or it was a slow night. Those guys were real characters. Those guys were major league characters. A lot of them were right out of Damon Runyon."
—Bill Rapp, Jr.,
Student Manager

The Clover Club was the meeting place for Syracuse athletes in the 1950s. Football was by far the king of all sports at Syracuse in 1959, and the football players dominated the scene at the Clover Club. Located on Almond street near the university, the Clover Club was the unofficial nightspot that was acceptable to the coaches for their athletes to gather. The legal drinking age in New York was 18, so going to places that served liquor was not off limits to most Syracuse students.

Off the field this '59 team was a mixed bunch, made up of many tough guys from diverse backgrounds. Players at Syracuse were expected to play with an attitude. Being hardnosed was a requirement or you didn't play. Many times those same traits carried over off the field. The Syracuse football players hung together and a tight bond existed amongst the entire team.

JOE SZOMBATHY (Assistant Coach): "When I was playing ball at Syracuse in 1953, a lot of the players went to the Clover Club. They had a Corned Beef sandwich specialty. They had built a hell of a business with the students. Their prices were cheap. They had no cover, no minimum, no nothing and you could dance in the back. It was a great hangout. Ben didn't have a problem with the players going there. He knew typical college kids had to go somewhere and he figured, "Hell if the players were in one place, that was good.""

MAURY YOUMANS (Tackle): "The Clover Club was located on the city's south side not far from the university. It was the bar for all of the ball players. Athletes from all sports went there, not just the football players. It was just a great college bar. It had a good jukebox and a dance floor with booths around it. A lot of time was spent on the bowling machine that you pushed a puck down. Roger Davis probably made a living on that, as well as playing cards. Irv, and Fooey were the bartenders, and they became personal friends of ours. I think that the most outstanding thing they served besides beer was peanut butter, pickle and banana sandwiches. How weird is that one?

"The place was our hangout and we were able to go there and not get bothered by anybody. The coaches knew we were there and they didn't have a problem with it, as long as we stayed out of trouble. You have to keep in mind that drinking was not really allowed on campus because Syracuse was a Methodist school, so in a way, you couldn't have any drinking on campus. This was our fraternity for ball players. You could do anything you wanted there. The girls obviously came where the guys were. Being young, red blooded young men we enjoyed the beer and the girls. It was just a great place to be."

BOB THOMAS (Quarterback): "The Clover club was a place you could go and for $1.25 get a steak, a salad and a beer. I use to take my girl Barbara there. We're still married 41 years later. Well, she detested the place. She said it was a crummy place to go. She liked the Tecumseh Club where the fraternity guys used to go to."

Swapping Clover Club stories 40 years later (left to right): Jim Lamey, John Howell, Gene Grabowski, and Al Gerlick. Courtesy of Gerhard Schwedes.

AL GERLICK (Tackle): "I loaned Bob Stem my car so he could take his girl home. He comes back and he wants to fight. He was all drunked up. He grabs me and starts to roll me over the bar. I said, 'Let's go outside.' I had this trench coat on and like a dummy, as we walked outside, I was unbuttoning my coat. Well, he pops me right in the nose. I went down in one shot. He buckled my knees. He almost killed me. Blood is everywhere. I said,'What are you doing? I just gave you my car to take your girlfriend home?' Luckily, Leon Cholakis was there. He says, 'Get out of here before the cops come.' You see I wasn't even supposed to be at the Clover Club that night. I was a proctor in the dorm and that was how I was getting my room and board. Later Stem called up and apologized. I still think that is why I had two operations, because he hit me flush in my nose. Oddly, that was probably the only fight I ever had. I always broke up fights. I was no fighter. I was a breaker upper and a lover, No, I wish I was a lover."

JERRY SKONIECKI (End): "The Clover Club was right up on Almond Street. Of all the places we had that were open to us, we hung

Jerry Skonieczki flexing his muscles. Courtesy of Pat Whelan.

around there. I mean it was the dirtiest, the dingiest place yet. Everybody and their mother from the area came down there because, it was like we were on display you know? And everybody wanted to rub elbows. It was our place. I remember a guy by the name of George De-Barber, who was a beer salesmen. He had a nice Chesterfield coat and a matching Hamborg, he always dressed to the nines, and we couldn't wait for him to get in there. He sold Carlings Black Label beer. Before we knew George, we were drinking Budweiser, Maybe Genesee, but when he got there he'd buy us Black Label. Oh, it was awful, but it was free. We drank it and we made that place one of the best Carlings Black Label locations in the area. The Clover Club had a piano up there on the stage and I remember going up there and playing it. It was a great place."

DICK EASTERLY (Quarterback): "One of the funny stories regarding the Clover Club was about Roger Davis. I was down there quite a bit and of course, Roger was down there. Roger liked to play cards and a lot of the time there was a card game going on in the back. There was a guy from Syracuse that had made All City in football. He played at Vocational and wanted to make a name for himself. I had played against him in high school, so I knew him a little bit. He wouldn't come around during the season but usually in the summertime, when he figured all the players were away from school. Anyway, he would come in about nine-thirty every night and say, 'Where is Roger? I want a piece of him.' You know I got sick of this after a couple of weeks so I told him, Look, if you want Roger, come in at eleven-thirty or twelve o'clock and he will be here. But the guy would never show up. I was telling Roger about this guy wanting a piece of him so Roger comes in one night early and we go meet the guy. I said, 'Here's Roger and he wants to talk to you.' The guy got all nervous and starts sweating, and he says, 'Geeze Roger, I just wanted to say to you how much I admire you.' That guy couldn't get out of there fast enough."

BOB YATES (Tackle): "Every now and then us old timers would have an old time dance (where I now live,) down here in Texas. I'd say to my wife, 'Oh, Oh, there's a Clover Club Song. I remember dancing to that when I was at the Clover Club.' "

ROGER DAVIS (Guard): "Jim Saylor, Pat Whalen and I were at the Clover Club and I kept using a term Pat didn't like. He said, 'If you do that again I'm going to whack you.' And he did. Then the next thing I knew, I had to separate him and Saylor from fighting each other, and I was the one who got hit. Another time we left the Clover Club and went to the Nedrow Tavern. We were there with the Indians. They were drinking and we were drinking. Dave Baker gets into an argument with one and I went to walk outside. I had never even talked to anybody and the guy thought I was Baker and tore my shirt off. He just ripped it right off my back. So naturally, I jumped on him and ended up having a fight in the parking lot at the Nedrow Tavern. The Indians were good to fight with, as it was just punching and that was all."

LEON CHOLAKIS (Tackle): "Everybody used to go there and get the pitchers of beer and the sandwiches, the Clover Club Specials. They had two or three specials. One that was popular was the peanut butter, mayonnaise and pickle sandwich. Irv and Fooey were bartenders and Sid was the owner. Upstairs they had the rooms they would rent to the guys who would live there for the summer."

AL BEMILLER (Center): "The Clover Club, Christ, that's where it all happened. The only place you could get away with throwing beer bottles. You break them and the next day you came, everything was all straightened out. If you needed money, they gave you money and you paid them the following week. It was great. We all went there. We never had any problems that I know of. That was our place."

JP BYRNE (Quintessential Fan/Friend. All 5'8" of him): "I had a tendency to get in trouble with my mouth and Roger, and all the guys really, always kept an eye on me. They made sure that I didn't get in too much trouble. Anyway there was a brawl at the Clover Club one night. I basically started it even though I was innocent in this particular situation. Somebody had brought flowers around, I believe roses. I was walking around and I had one hanging in my mouth. I'm over in the corner and suddenly these three guys come up to me. These guys had just finished Marine Boot Camp. So they decided to venture into the Clover Club, which was probably not smart idea to begin with, looking for trouble. They spotted me and they figured I'm the one to beat on. So I turned around and I started back toward the bar. I know Cannonball(Al Gerlick), John Howell, and Freddy Hilliard are there. I said, I got these three guys here who want to kick my ass. Anyway the thing wound up outside, and I can remember, it was Howell who was a very tough guy, just took one guy apart. Freddy Hilliard had a raincoat on and somebody had grabbed him from behind, trying to stop him, and the raincoat ripped right up the back. It was just one of these old time brawls. We wound up discussing it at the diner somewhere downtown afterwards. All I got from Hilliard was, 'JP you Bastard, look at my raincoat.' Because it got ripped up the back it was my fault. It was just a crazy night."

JOHN BROWN (Tackle): "I would go down to the Clover Club. A $1.25 steak and a pitcher of beer for 75 cents. The comradery of the players, plus the guys who owned it really made it great. If you didn't have the dollar and a quarter it didn't matter because they would feed you anyway."

DAVE BAKER (End): "I was only down there about once a month. (Laughter) I thought it more of a intellectual place. (More laughter) We'd go down there and we'd have a streak dinner and some times even cook it ourselves on the grill. I'd go up and play the piano on the stage. I used to play by ear, so I could play the piano. When I was injured, I really didn't feel that I could just watch the guys play, so

"How about a game of basketball?" (back row, left to right): Maury Youmans, Gerhard Schwedes, Roger Davis, Ron Bartlett, and Pat Whelan; (kneeling, left to right): Jim Anderson, Jerry Skonieczki, and Jim Saylor. Courtesy of Gerhard Schwedes.

I'd go down to the Clover Club and we would listen to the game on the radio. They really didn't have TV coverage like they have TV coverage today. It was tough listening to the games."

DAVE APPELHOF (Center): "I enjoyed the Tecumseh Club, it wasn't a hole in the ground like the Clover Club was."

DICK BEYER (Assistant Coach): "I went down to the Clover Club not to hang out with the players, but because Ben wanted to make sure that there wasn't any trouble, any fights or anything like that. If there was, then it effects the whole team and I don't remember anything that happened."

Fred Mautino, "The Chief," coming up big against Penn
State. Courtesy of Syracuse University Archives.

15

Penn State

Columbia professor Charles VanDoren was big news as Syracuse and Penn State began preparing for Saturday's epic battle. VanDoren, who had won $129,000 dollars on the now-defunct game show *Twenty-One*, admitted to the House Subcommittee that the producer of the show, Albert Freedman, provided him answers to questions on each of his fourteen appearances on the show. "I have deceived my friends, and I had millions of them," VanDoren told committee members.

VanDoren's troubles were no concern to Ben Schwartzwalder and Rip Engle. They had their own problems. Both, like VanDoren, were looking for guaranteed answers on how to beat the other fellow. Each coach, fiercely competitive by nature, was aware of the magnitude of the contest and tried to downplay the "game of the year" in the East. This one was for all the marbles! One of these teams would move on to a major bowl bid and a possible national championship; the other would end a story book year.

Engle's team had exceeded his expectations by far. He had never imagined at the beginning of the season that this group would be undefeated going into the Syracuse game. Blessed with a wonderful leader in quarterback Richie Lucas, Engle was confident his team would play well against Syracuse. This team had a way of getting it done; there was no quit in any of them.

RIP ENGLE (Penn State Head Coach): "I'm not saying we can't be licked but this team doesn't scare easily. We're going after it. You never know what will happen. We'll come up with something that may work."

Whatever Rip had planned, he made sure Syracuse wasn't going to find out about it. Engle posted guards around Beaver Stadium to make sure no uninvited guests observed Penn State's practices. Engle this season had installed a new offense, a "double-winged-T," with the halfbacks in the slots. He felt it gave his team more plays to run without making it too complicated for the players. He felt with the type of personnel he had on this year's team this type of offense would utilize their skills best.

JOE SZOMBATHY (Assistant Coach): "Richie Lucas is so effective in roll-outs and passes, this double-winged-T is a most difficult offense to defend. By placing his backs in the slots behind the tackles, Penn State is able to run a reverse trap off Lucas's roll-outs. It's their misdirection play, and our defense had better be ready for it, they run it very well."

Richie Lucas was called by his head coach, "The best player I have ever coached." The senior quarterback was also an outstanding defender and led the Nittany Lions in interceptions. A capable passer, Lucas was probably the best ball-faker in the country. Running wide on the option play, he had the ability to seemingly always make the right decision on whether to keep the ball or pitch to the trailing back. He was a cool customer, a leader on the team. He told Rip Engle, "Coach, don't worry about this game, our guys will do what they're supposed to do. Syracuse, they're going to have to show us they're that good." Lucas wasn't being cocky. He was just an athlete who played they game hard and believed in himself and in his teammates, the mark of a great leader.

JOE PATERNO (Penn State Assistant Coach): "Illinois this year was inside the 10-yard line, second down. They ran a play to the left and Lucas made the tackle. They ran a play to the right and Lucas made the tackle. Then they run a play up the middle and Lucas is there to help. He's the best football player I ever saw."

BEN SCHWARTZWALDER: "Rip Engle has the most imaginative offense of any team we've played. We've not only got to stop roll-outs and outside stuff but we also know that they can hurt anybody up the middle. Even if we hold them on the ground we've got to cope with fine passing by Richie Lucas and sophomore Galen Hall."

Schwartzwalder was now besieged by national writers wanting to know more about his powerhouse team. One writer asked him, "Ben, do you allow yourself after six games to compare this team to others that you have coached at Syracuse?"

Schwartzwalder, fidgeting and fooling with his glasses, answered, "I'd rather it was after seven games. Uh, so far, if nothing happens, the line has been solid so far." Schwartzwalder was not about to say anything glowing about his team with his arch-enemy Rip Engle listening. It was tough enough going down there to play at Penn State; the last thing he wanted was he or his team to appear cocky.

The weather in upstate New York had not been cooperative and Syracuse was forced to practice indoors. "It snowed yesterday and we had twenty-seven days of rain last month," Schwartzwalder said in frustration. Ben was complimentary of Penn State and rightly so. This was the best team Syracuse would play so far this season. Schwartzwalder knew Engle would have his boys ready, and not being able to practice outside was a concern.

"Spirit Week" was the name given by the Penn State rooters to the week preceding their encounter with Syracuse in an effort to get the students psyched up for the game. Signs all over the campus offered encouragement to their beloved Nittany Lions. "Beat Syracuse" and "Squeeze the Orange" were seen everywhere. Tickets to the 31,000-seat Beaver Stadium had been sold out for weeks. The ticket office gave a ray of hope to students without tickets by announcing on Friday that a few hundred standing-room-only tickets would go on sale for $2 each. These half-priced tickets would be the last chance to be in the stadium on Saturday. Scalpers were reportedly getting the unheard-of sum of $60 per ticket.

Syracuse students were just as excited and many planned to car pool down to University Park for the game whether they had tickets or not. A few overzealous Syracuse fans had already traveled down to Penn State on Monday to paint an Orange circle around the eye of the Nittany Lion, whose statue stood in front of Beaver Stadium. Syracuse players were equally excited about the upcoming game and protested loudly when the coaching staff decided to hold practice indoors because of the swirling snow. One Syracuse player who had added incentive to beat Penn State was reserve tackle Gene Grabowsky. A native of nearby Liverpool, Grabowsky had attended Penn State as a freshmen in 1956. The 6'6", 265-pound lineman had injured his back so badly during the frosh football season that the doctors at Penn State didn't think he would ever be able to play football again. Penn State no longer wanted Grabowsky and he transferred to Syracuse. Redshirted last season, the 'big fella' was aching to get a crack at his old team who had given up on him.

GENE GRABOWSKY (Tackle): "I'll jump up and down and spit nickels if we beat Penn State."

JIM ANDERSON (Halfback): "We were sitting in front of the gym before practice on the steps there. A couple of guys were trying to bounce this car, get the back wheels up. Gene went over by himself, lifted the damned thing up in the air, and dropped it back down. Boy is he strong."

The Associated Press still had the Orangemen at number four, but the UPI poll had moved the Orangemen up to number three. The Nittany Lions continued to maintain their number seven position in both polls. LSU, who came back to defeat Mississippi, 7–3, on a fourth-quarter, 89-yard punt return by halfback Billy Cannon, remained at number one. The Tigers would travel to Tennessee Saturday in what would be their last tough game of the season. The number two ranked team in the country, Northwestern, would face once-beaten Wisconsin in a battle for first place in the Big Ten. Texas. one place ahead of Syracuse in the AP, would entertain the Baylor Bears.

The winner of the Syracuse/Penn State contest on Saturday was projected to be offered a spot in the Orange Bowl. With LSU primed to run the table again and go undefeated, their Sugar Bowl invitation looked assured. Northwestern, with a win on Saturday over Wisconsin, would take a big step forward toward the Rose Bowl and a date with undefeated Southern California in Pasadena on New Year's day. Texas, the leader in the Southwest Conference, looked very strong, and seemed to be headed for the Cotton Bowl.

The only bowl game reported in the Associated Press not available to the Penn State/Syracuse winner was the Sugar Bowl. Because both teams had Negro players, it was reported, "This would cause complications." Neither team would have accepted that type of attitude, but the Sugar Bowl or any other bowl was the farthest thing from their minds as they prepared to face each other.

Syracuse, for the first time this year, would be playing a team with equal talent. Penn State could match Syracuse in depth and came into the game fairly healthy. Lucas, last week in the win over West Virginia, had been knocked out in the second quarter and did not return. In his absence, Galen Hall threw for one touchdown and demonstrated why he was rated the top quarterback coming out of high school two years before. Lucas practiced all week and looked ready to go against Syracuse.

Beaver Stadium was filled to the brim as Syracuse co-captains Gerhard Schwedes and Whitey Reimer walked out to midfield for the coin toss. Syracuse, in their white jerseys with blue trim, orange pants, and orange helmets, won the toss and elected to receive. Ernie Davis took the opening kickoff at the Syracuse 10-yard line, cut upfield, found a small opening to his right, and returned the ball to the Syracuse 25. On first down the Orange ran a screen pass to Davis who motored 14 yards upfield for a first down. Fullback Art Baker, off-tackle, gained 8 yards as the Syracuse line opened a big hole in the Lion defense. On second down, running right, Dave Sarette pitched to Schwedes who rambled to the Penn State 39.

Over on the home team's sidelines, Engle signaled for a timeout. Engle wanted to slow the game. Syracuse had the early momentum and he wanted his players to regroup and settle down. Syracuse, after the timeout, went back to Schwedes on a pitch out. Again running right, Schwedes turned the corner and sprinted 11 yards for another first down. Unfortunately for Syracuse they were flagged for holding and pushed back 15 yards. Sarette, attempting to pass on two successive plays, could not find an open man and the visitors were forced to punt.

Penn State, starting on their own 21, gained 11 yards on two running plays to get a first down at the Penn State 32-yard line. After Lion fullback Botula gained 8 yards, Lucas got loose on a roll-out and scampered 16 yards to the Syracuse 44-yard line. On first down Lucas found halfback Dick Hoak alone at the Syracuse goal line. Hitting the wide-open Hoak perfectly, the senior back dropped the ball. On fourth down Engle decided to go for it. With the Lions setting up in their punt formation, Lucas ran head-on into Syracuse defensive back Ed Bowers at the 36-yard line, falling one yard short of the first down, and Syracuse took over on downs.

After moving the ball to the Lion 45-yard line, Sarette, running wide on third down, was hit hard by Lion tackle Andy Stynchula, fumbled, and Richie Lucas pounced on the loose ball at the Penn State 46.

Lucas, running wide on first down, gained 9 yards to the Syracuse 37. On second down Lucas found Hoak wide open again at the Orange 22. This time Hoak hung on to the pigskin to give Penn State another first down deep in Syracuse territory. After pushing the ball to the Syracuse 17-yard line, sophomore running back Roger Kochman burst up the middle of the Syracuse defense and sprinted into the end zone for the game's first score. The extra point went wide right but Penn State led, 6–0.

Sarette, staying in the game to quarterback the second unit, moved the team downfield, reaching the Penn State 14-yard line as the first quarter ended. On the first play of the second quarter, Sarette threw into the end zone but was intercepted by Hoak who returned the ball to his 7-yard line before being tackled by Al Gerlick. The Lions picked up an important first down moving out to the 21-yard line before punting. Under a heavy Syracuse rush, Lucas barely got the kick off, which weakly went out of bounds at the State 43.

Schwartzwalder decided to stay on the ground and Syracuse backs Baker and Schwedes gained 21 yards on two runs to give the Orange a first down at the Penn State 22. After a clipping penalty moved Syracuse back, Sarette found Fred Mautino open at the Lion 18-yard line. The big end caught the ball between two State defenders and was finally knocked out of bounds at the Lions' 11-yard line. Davis ran off-tackle for 5 yards. Schwedes then took Sarette's pitch and sped into the end zone for the touchdown. Yates' kick put Syracuse in the lead, 7–6. Beaver Stadium, for the first time all afternoon, was quiet.

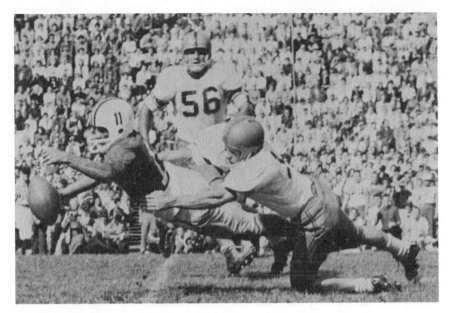

Stopping Penn State's quarterback, Richie Lucas from getting a first down.
Courtesy of Syracuse University Archives.

Penn State came roaring back and moved into Orange territory off
the fancy running of Lucas. Rolling out again from his 36-yard line,
the Lion All-American avoided being sacked as four Syracuse defenders
had their hands on him. Lucas, finally finding some daylight, sprinted
down the field before Mark Weber corralled him at the Syracuse 35.
On the ensuing first down, Mautino broke through the line sacking
Lucas for a 10-yard loss. The Nittany Lions, after two running plays,
punted. Every player on both sides of the field were giving all that they
had to give and the hitting between the two teams was the fiercest of
the year.

Syracuse and Penn State exchanged punts as the first half ended
with Mautino again sacking Lucas in the Lions' last possession, this
time for a 15-yard loss. The Syracuse all-purpose end, nicknamed "The
Big Chief," was making his presence known on both sides of the ball.

Starting the second half Penn State gained one first down before
Syracuse's crashing ends, Mautino and Jerry Skonieczki, sacked Lucas
on consecutive plays forcing Penn State to punt.

Syracuse started from their own 44-yard line. Baker gained 12 yards off tackle. After Baker and Sarette gained 9 yards on two running plays, Schwedes went off-tackle and fought forward to the State 29 and a first down. Davis gained 6 yards on the scissors before Sarette, running the ride series, ran 13 yards to the Lion 10-yard line. After moving the ball to the State 5-yard line, Sarette found Baker in the back of the end zone for the touchdown. Yates' conversion put Syracuse ahead, 14–6, and that was the way the score remained starting the fourth quarter.

Penn State's first drive in the last period stalled as they were hit with a personal foul penalty. Bob Mitinger's poor punt gave Syracuse great field position at the Lion 41. Nine straight running plays found Davis pounding over from the 3-yard line to extend the Syracuse lead to 20–6. Yates missed the extra point but Syracuse had very quickly taken control of the game. Nittany Lion fans were becoming restless. Their team needed something to happen to get back in this game.

Yates' kickoff reached the Lions' goal line where Kochman caught the ball. Immediately swerving to his right, the Pennsylvania sprint champion found a huge gap on the sideline. With Skonieczki and Mautino desperately trying catch him, Kochman raced 100 yards for the touchdown. Penn State, who only a few seconds ago appeared out of the game, found new life now trailing 20–12. Engle went for 2 points with Lucas rolling right but the State quarterback threw too low for the diving Hoak to make the reception. There were eleven minutes to play in the game and the Lions now trailed only by 8 points.

After exchanging possessions again, Lucas's punt rolled dead at the Syracuse 10-yard line. The Syracuse offense, now being shut down by the fired up Lion defense, gained 9 yards on three running plays and was again forced to punt. Yates took the snap from center Bemiller and prepared to kick as tackle Andy Stynchula broke in from the right side. Going airborne over two Syracuse blockers, Stynchula extended his arms and reached as high as he possibly could making contact with the ball and sending it bouncing crazily into a pile of players. Both teams, diving for the football, pushed the elusive pigskin to the Syracuse 1-yard line where Penn State recovered. Beaver Stadium was now rocking. State fans, who only a few minutes before were silent, were now delirious. Syracuse fans and players were stunned. Their lead , apparently insurmountable only a few minutes before, had dissipated and now Penn State was lining up to score again.

On first down the Lions' halfback, Sam Sobczak, scored to close the gap to 20–18. Syracuse, with their second defensive line in the game, braced for the biggest play of the season. A successful two-point conversion by Penn State would tie the game. Along the front line Gerlick, Cholokis, Grabowsky, and Bob Stem dug in knowing the weight of the season was on their shoulders. Somehow this group of young men had to come up with a play: This whole wonderful season was riding on it.

Penn State came out of the huddle sending Hoak wide right to the near sideline. Lucas, over center and barking out signals, took the snap and handed off to super sophomore Kochman. Syracuse, in a six-man line, charged forward, each lineman staying low, digging, digging, trying to push Penn State's big linemen backwards. Kochman, taking the handoff with no visible opening, dove into the pile and was lost in a sea of humanity. The referees quickly moved in, slowly untangling the players. As player by player was pulled from the pile, Beaver Stadium was eerily silent. State fans prayed that their young star had reached the goal line. As the last few players were pulled off the pile it became clear Kochman had been stopped. Gene Grabowsky, the former Nittany Lion, had made the play of the year. 'Gino' had gotten his revenge! Syracuse had held and still led, 20–18, with less than five minutes to play.

Syracuse sent Davis and Schwedes back deep for the kickoff. Penn State's end-over-end kickoff sailed toward the right sideline where Davis, running hard to catch the ball, mistook the restraining line as the sideline and was ruled out-of-bounds deep in Orange territory at the 6-yard line. The young back had made a major error in judgement and his team was again backed up to the goal line.

On the sideline, Ben Schwartzwalder called his first group together. Here was the game. The whole season was right now. He needed to get his team back on track; they needed to regain their composure.

Schwartzwalder, speaking as loudly as he could in an effort to be heard over the frenzied crowd, told his players, "All right boys, lets look at the facts. You're a fine football team and you've played a fine football game. Now I'll go beyond that—you're a great football team, but you're going to have to prove it for four and a half minutes. You will prove it! Now go out there and do it."

Syracuse never relinquished the ball, marching 53 yards down the field and running out the clock. Syracuse had withstood a great Penn State comeback. The Nittany Lions had scored 12 points in the fourth quarter but couldn't stop Syracuse's offense when they needed to.

RICHIE LUCAS (Penn State Quarterback): "Each team going into that game was undefeated. We were both ranked in the top five in the nation at the time. I thought we had the advantage because we were playing at home. A couple things come to mine. First we lost 20–18 so we didn't make any extra points. Also, Andy Stynchula blocking a punt and giving us the momentum late in the game. Then Syracuse just ran the ball down our throats. We played our hearts out as did Syracuse. The fans gave both teams a standing ovation which I thought said something about the Penn State fans and the game itself."

RIP ENGLE (Penn State Head Coach): "Syracuse has the greatest running offense of any team we have ever played against. Their backs are all big and strong . . . and they have such terrific balance, they are tough to stop. They have a fine team . . . one of the finest I have ever seen."

BEN SCHWARTZWALDER: "That Richie Lucas is the greatest we have played against. He's a real All-American. That Kochman kid is a great kid too."

Rip Engle, gracious in defeat, came to the Syracuse locker room where he told the Orange players they had a great team and hoped they went a long, long way this season.

JOE SZOMBATHY (Assistant Coach): "Ben had frozen his feet in the war so he always had cold feet. I remember we went to an Army-Navy store the morning of the Penn State game and he bought these big, heavy shoes that he wore on the sidelines. Ben didn't give a shit how he looked on the sidelines. Christ, his hat would be crooked, he'd have his pants down low. He just didn't care. He was too engrossed in the game."

MAURY YOUMANS (Tackle): "Andy Stynchula from Penn State was the toughest player we faced. He's the one that blocked that punt on us. He came up over Schwedes and me to block that punt near the end zone. I remember Andy going in the air like he was Superman. He just flew over the top of us. He was tough."

DAVE APPELHOF (Center): "When Penn State came on the field just before the game, the crowd exploded for Penn State. It sent a chill up my spine. I'll never forget that. It was a great thrill."

MAURY YOUMANS (Tackle): "I remember that last drive against Penn State well. We were tired, we were hot, but we were determined. There was always somebody to inspire you in a huddle. Gerhard was always 100% in the game. He might be dead tired, or had just ran out for two or three pass routes in a row, but he would always come back to the huddle, full of fire, ready to go again. Things like that keep everybody going. I remember just being very inspired in that drive to make sure that we opened holes. That five minutes we were a very determined team. That was the season, that drive."

VAL PINCHBACK (Syracuse Sports Information Director, 1959): "I remember when we played Penn State in that 20–18 game, CBS did the game. Chris Schenkel was doing the game for CBS. I was down on the field when the players came out, Roger Davis, Gene Grabowski, and I remember Chris Schenkel turning to me and saying, 'They're bigger than the Giants.' It was those kind of things that got us around to calling the line 'The Sizeable Seven.' I think those things lend itself to creating something."

Richie LUCAS

PENN STATE QUARTERBACK

Our team wasn't particularly close but there was an old saying, 'Once you put the jock strap on, you became a different person.' Once we got dressed and went to the practice field, we became a football team. We called Rip (Rip Engle) 'The Great Grandfather.' Back in those days Eastern football was, well, Eastern football, with Pittsburgh, Penn State, Syracuse, West Virginia, and Army and Navy time to time. There was an animosity with the fans about the other schools. That wasn't true with the coaches, though.

"Joe Paterno was one of our assistants back then. He was young at the time, but players never thought about that, they only thought about the responsibilities that go with the title. I knew Joe would be a good head coach, but I don't think anyone would project what he would accomplish."

Richie Lucas, Penn State Quarterback. Courtesy of Richie Lucas.

"In your dreams!" Courtesy of Syracuse University Archives.

16

Colgate

As the Syracuse players rejoiced in their locker room in Beaver Stadium over their hard-fought victory over Penn State, the word came down that number one LSU and number two Northwestern had lost. The ecstatic players realized they were now number one!

LSU, after nineteen straight wins and fourteen weeks as the nation's top team, had just lost to Tennessee, 14–13. The Tigers had been stopped on a two-point conversion attempt which ended up being the difference in the game. Northwestern, losing 24–19, was outclassed by Wisconsin and their outstanding quarterback Dale Hackbart. The once-beaten Badgers now had the inside track for the Rose Bowl, possibly leaving Northwestern out in the cold come New Year's Day.

Ben Schwartzwalder and Rip Engle, never considered friends, were lavish in their praise of each other and how well both teams had played. Schwartzwalder knew his team had dodged a bullet. He was so proud of the players and their ability to elevate their play when called upon to do so. This was by far the best group of players he had ever coached. His second-team defense had saved the season with that goal line stop of the Lions' two-point conversion.

Penn State now behind him, Ben Schwartzwalder looked to get his team ready for the Colgate Red Raiders while dealing with the pressures of coaching the number one team in the nation.

The signing of the "Cazenovia Pact" was the kickoff for the big social weekend that accompanied the Colgate-Syracuse rivalry. Once the Pact was signed, it was open season on getting scalps. Students from both schools would now make raids on each other's campus in search of some unsuspecting student who they could capture, than shave a big "S" or "C" in their hair. Some Syracuse coeds were relentless in their "razor raids" of Colgate men, and once they captured their prey, it was all over, those guys were sporting a big "S." Each of Syracuse's sororities and fraternities held contests for the best posters depicting the rivalry and Colgate's demise, and the winning placards would be prominently displayed outside each of the Greek houses. The pep rally on Friday night introduced the "Colgate Queen and her court," followed by rousing talks from Dean Noble and Coach Schwartzwalder. Spirit ran high on Friday night and many times following the pep rally, panty raids were made on the coeds' dorms.

The students at Syracuse started celebrating earlier in the week when their beloved Orangemen were named number one in the nation by both the AP and UPI. Hearing the news, students stormed out into the streets, car horns honked, strangers embraced, the whole campus engulfed with people. Deciding to head downtown, a wild parade ensued with thousands of students marching down Salina Street waving signs proclaiming Syracuse number one in the nation. The partying would last long into the night.

The Orangemen, besides becoming the nation's number one team, also became the principal team to recruit by the bowl committees across the country. The Orange Bowl quickly extended an offer to Syracuse to come to Miami again as did the new kid on the block, the Liberty Bowl. Syracuse's Athletic Board met to discuss the bowl situation but no decision was made at that point. The Board wanted to hear from the players where they would like to play and also wait to see if the Cotton Bowl was going to extend an invitation. The Cotton Bowl, very interested in Syracuse, decided not to make any formal offers until after next week's games.

The players met to discuss what bowl they would prefer. Schwartzwalder had told the team before the meeting that they would ultimately decide on where they would like to play, not him or the Athletic

Board. The decision was to be theirs. The players quickly choose the Orange Bowl.

This decision created a firestorm across the country. With Texas the nation's number two team and the obvious choice for the Cotton Bowl, many people envisioned them taking on number one Syracuse for the national championship. It was a natural. Newspaper articles across the country wrote that the Syracuse players were afraid of Texas, that it was their duty to take on the best opponent. Letters in the local Syracuse newspapers begged the players to reconsider. They had proven all year that they were great, and now Syracuse fans wanted their team to play the best opponent that college football had to offer. The players weren't ducking any team; they just liked and preferred the Orange Bowl. The Athletic Board through all this fuss remained quiet.

GERHARD SCHWEDES (Halfback): "We had confidence. We didn't care about who we were playing, or where we played. It didn't matter. At that point we knew that we were going to win the ball game. In our minds we'd have beaten the Green Bay Packers that year, that's how strong we believed in ourselves."

The Colgate game against the Orange would be the sixtieth meeting of these two schools, beginning way back in 1896. The Red Raiders had last beat Syracuse in 1950, 19–14, and had lost eight straight coming into the '59 game. Surprisingly, Colgate still held the advantage in the series, 31–23–5. Colgate coach Alva Kelley had a tall task ahead preparing his 1–5 team to battle the undefeated Orangemen.

ALVA KELLEY (Colgate Head Coach): "I look at it as a privilege to play against such a team. The only way you can get the true measure of a man is to send him up against the best there is. Our boys will certainly get their opportunity this weekend."

Alva Kelley, in his first year at Colgate, was trying to rebuild a program that had hit tough times. Summoned from Brown University, Kelley knew he was short on talent, but through positive reenforcement, he kept his players' attitude up. Kelley stressed working hard, taking one game at a time, never being overly critical of his player. He knew it would be at least a couple years before Colgate would be competitive.

The Red Raiders, a seven-touchdown underdog, were led by junior running back Jacque MacKinnon. In the 1957 freshmen game against Syracuse, he scored four touchdowns in leading Colgate to victory.

BEN SCHWARTZWALDER: "It's nice to have the team get all this recognition but our job is to get ready for Colgate. That MacKinnon does everything well. He runs hard and with speed, and he can catch a pass. We'll have to watch that boy closely."

JIM SHREVE (Freshmen Coach): "Colgate is a vastly improved team. They played a real good game against Holy Cross, and I'd say they are 100 percent better now than they were at the beginning of the season."

As the week went by, the Orange Bowl Committee tried to get Syracuse to commit to playing in Miami on New Year's Day. Stating that they were concerned that if they waited on Syracuse, and they said no, that it might then be too late for the Orange Bowl to get another quality team. The Orange Bowl might be forced to withdraw their invitation to Syracuse and invite another team.

Syracuse didn't budge to the pressure so the Orange Bowl committee retracted their statement and said they would wait for Syracuse to make a decision.

Thirty thousand fans, most dressed in orange, showed up to cheer their top-ranked team and say good-bye to the seventeen seniors playing their last game in Archbold Stadium. Al Smith, the venerable public address announcer, introduced the Orangemen slightly differently this day as the home team raced onto the field. The always understated Smith said, "The Orangemen from Syracuse . . . the number one team in the nation." The rain drenched crowd stood and cheered.

Colgate, on offense first, fumbled the second play from scrimmage and Bob Yates pounced on the ball at the Red Raider 28-yard line. Two plays later Dave Sarette hit Gerhard Schwedes on a 30-yard pass for the touchdown. Yates kick made it 7–0 and the slaughter was on. Syracuse would score three more times in the first period, leading 30–0 as the first quarter came to a close. Colgate kept fumbling and Syracuse kept scoring.

Schwartzwalder, freely substituting, watched as his team kept pouring it on. In the fourth period, leading 51–0, Schwartzwalder put

Pete Brokaw gets loose against Colgate. Courtesy of Syracuse University Archives.

Ernie Davis back into the game with the third team. Davis, taking a quick pitch, ran right, and seeing no room to run, stopped, then started running to his left. Picking up a sea of blockers, the sophomore tailback sprinted 56 yards for the score.

When it was finally over, Syracuse had defeated Colgate 71–0. The Orangemen had gained 438 yards rushing and scored 10 touchdowns, six of which were by air. The Red Raiders fumbled ten times and returned eleven kickoffs in the game, still records of futility forty-four years later. Speaking of forty-four, Davis had eighty-eight yards on six carries. Backup quarterback Dick Easterly completed six of nine passes for 114 yards and three touchdowns. Sophomore Pete Brokaw, getting some extended playing time at his new halfback position, caught four passes for 114 yards and one touchdown, and was voted the game's best back. Senior Al Gerlick, in his last home game, was voted the best lineman by the press.

Following the game, Syracuse announced it had been offered and accepted a bid to play in the Cotton Bowl. The Syracuse players had apparently changed their minds about going to the Orange Bowl.

MAURY YOUMANS (Tackle): "We had a team meeting when it was decision time for which bowl we were going to in '59. Coach called us together and he said. 'Boys, all the bowls want you.' And then he said, 'I'm gonna let you guys select the bowl you want to go to, but the only thing that I want you to keep in mind is that Texas is number two and they're going to the Cotton Bowl.' We were ranked number one at the time. Then he and the coaches walked out.

"We immediately voted for the Orange Bowl. We had been there last year and loved Florida, Miami in particular. The hell with who is number two, we just wanted to go down and have a good time. We felt at that time we could beat anybody. So we called the coaches back in. Gerhard, as our Captain said, 'Coach, we voted for the Orange Bowl.' Ben, as he had a way of doing, looked over his glasses, rather than through them and said, 'Boys, I think you had better vote again,' turned around and walked out. We all voted for the Cotton Bowl."

BEN SCHWARTZWALDER: "At halftime (45–0) I told the boys to go out and play some more football. We came to play a football game and we wanted the kids to play their best all the way. I believe you should play football all out or not at all. You've got to keep hustling out there or somebody gets hurt."

ALVA KELLEY (Colgate Head Coach): "They're a tremendous, wonderful ball club, and I certainly would agree with their number one ranking. Their defense is cleverly conceived and terrifically executed. They're a great team and the finest team I have ever coached against."

MAURY YOUMANS (Tackle): "Jerry Skonieczki and I would line up on the kickoff team next to each other. We had this 'rah rah' thing between us. It was basically put on, but I would shake my fist and I would say, 'Let's go, Jerry,' and he would go, 'Let's go, Maury,' and then we would run down hard, racing each other, as the kick was made. I remember in the Colgate game taking my eyes off of the blocker and cutting over to the right, because that's where the ball carrier was going. The next thing I know I was looking up at the sky. This guy just flattened me, and all I could think of, my immediate thought was, 'God, I hope that's not on the films, especially against Colgate.' Thank God it wasn't and I was very relieved.

"There is a great story that happened when we played Colgate. There was a bar in Dewitt called Walter White's, and the bartender, Jack Casey, who was a friend of mine had a running bet with a patron there. Jack would take Syracuse and the patron would take whoever we played. Well, Jack was becoming embarrassed since we had won every game that year, Jack had won every bet. So, going into the Colgate game, as he explained the story to me later, he told the guy, 'Im feeling guilty about winning all the time. I'll tell you what,' he said, 'I'll give you 70 points.' We beat Colgate 71–0 and I'll swear if that guy ever bet again he was foolish because when you can get 70 points in a football game and lose, you have no business ever making another bet."

Power sweep against Boston University. Courtesy of Gerhard Schwedes.

17

Boston University

Syracuse, now 8–0 on the season, was all set on their Bowl plans, but they wouldn't know who their opponent would be until Thanksgiving Day. Number two-ranked Texas had been upset the previous Saturday by TCU. The Longhorns now faced a must win against their last opponent, Texas A&M, to win the Southwest Conference Championship and receive a bid to the Cotton Bowl. The Arkansas Razorbacks were waiting in the wings if Texas stumbled against the Aggies. Schwartzwalder made plans to see the Longhorns in person on Thanksgiving day.

The Orangemen garnered 126 first place votes to take a commanding lead in the National Polls. Once beaten Mississippi moved up to number two in the voting, followed by LSU, Southern California, and Texas. Penn State remained at number seven and TCU, with their big win over Texas, moved to number ten in the nation. The Syracuse players were rightfully excited about being on the best team in the nation but understood there was still more football to be played.

DICK EASTERLY (Quarterback): "We've got to work all the harder now to maintain our standing."

GERRY SKONIECZKI (End): "It's the greatest. We've got something that will stay with us the rest of our lives. We played on the first Syracuse team ever to be rated first in the nation."

ERNIE DAVIS (Halfback): "Well, I can only hope we can go all the way and win the National Championship."

Second team leader, tackle Al Gerlick, was proud of his unit's huge contribution to the team's success and continued to beat the drum for more recognition for his boys, "Gerlick's Gorillas." "Cannonball," aptly named for his close proximity to the ground, was a real leader on the team. He was someone everyone respected and liked. When the press would rave on about the "Sizeable Seven," it was Al that would properly remind the fourth estate about the "Unnoticed Seven." The depth of the Syracuse team was remarkable.

Boston University Head Coach Steve Sinko was well aware of the strength Syracuse possessed.

STEVE SINKO (Boston University Head Coach): "I saw Syracuse in its opening game against Kansas, and I told people here in Boston that I didn't know who could beat them. I still don't think anybody is going to. We'll be trying though . . . we have a lot of red-blooded youngsters here. Everyone likes to test himself against the best and I know our boys will be going all out."

Boston University was 5–3 for the season, having just beaten arch rival Boston College, 26–7. The Terriers were beginning to play their best football of the season and had recently played Penn State very close for three quarters before losing 21–12.

BEN SCHWARTZWALDER: "We'd had better root for rain this Saturday, because this Boston U. Outfit can be real tough on a dry field. Our scouts say they played a good game against a pretty good Boston College team."

Steve Sinko's backfield, although not very big, possessed great speed. Halfbacks Paul Cancro and Hugh Bolin, a pair of 5'8", 175-pound speedsters, were very agile and tough to bring down in the open field. Both provided excellent targets for quarterback Emo DiNitto. DiNitto, an accurate passer, had thrown for 11 touchdown passes so far this season. Operating out of an unbalanced line, Sinko liked to split his ends wide while moving his speedy backs into the slots on many of their formations. BU's front line was one of the biggest Syracuse would face this year.

Ben Schwartzwalder got his wish. Rain filled the air as both teams

The Syracuse second team, "Gerlick's Gorillas." Front row (left to right): Tom Gilburg, John Brown, Al Gerlick, Otis Godfrey, Dave Appelhof, Dick Feidler, Ken Ericson; back row: Coach Bell, Dick Reimer, John Nichols, Dick Easterly, Mark Weber. Courtesy of Al Gerlick.

lined up for the kickoff at Boston University Stadium. Fred Mautino took a short kickoff and returned the ball to the Syracuse 37-yard line. The Orangemen, on a very muddy turf, moved the ball down the field with Ernie Davis, Art Baker, and Gerhard Schwedes carrying the ball in succession. Reaching the Terrier's 17-yard line, Dave Sarette rolled out, tossing a beautiful spiral to the back of the end zone where Schwedes made a leaping catch for the touchdown. The six play drive took just a shade over three minutes to complete. Bob Yates' extra point attempt was blocked, and Syracuse led 6–0.

The Terriers, on their first series, held to no yards, were forced to punt. The Orange, following the punt, drove down field reaching the BU 39-yard line. Running the scissors play, Ernie Davis fumbled and the Terriers recovered. For the rest of the quarter the teams exchanged punts .

Halfway through the second period Syracuse's first team mounted a drive, cleverly mixing a series of runs and short passes. Syracuse drove deep into BU territory, culminated by Ernie Davis going off tackle from the 5-yard line for the touchdown. Leading 12–0, Syracuse went for two, but Sarette, finding nobody open, was sacked.

Although BU was trailing in the game, the Terriers were doing a good job of slowing down the Syracuse scoring machine and created two more Syracuse turnovers on pass interceptions as the first half came to a close. A very angry Ben Schwartzwalder trudged toward his team's locker room where upon his arrival refused to go in. His team, a four touchdown favorite, had looked lousy, probably the worst that they had looked all season long. Ben told Rocco Pirro, 'You talk to them Rock, I'm thoroughly disgusted.' Rock went in, and when the team came on the field for the second half, they appeared ready to go.

Boston University took the second half kickoff and on three straight plays were pushed backwards by the now fired up Orange defense. Backed up near their goal line the Terriers first punt of the second half traveled only 30 yards going out of bounds at the BU 41-yard line. Syracuse only needed one play to score as Schwedes burst through the left side and outran two defenders to the goal line. A bad pass from center ruined the extra point, but Syracuse led 18–0.

The Orangemen would break the game wide open with one score in the third period and three more touchdowns in the last quarter. Fired up in the second half, the Syracuse defense totally shutdown the Terriers' offense and had two interceptions, the last being an Al Bemiller deflection that Ernie Davis returned untouched for a score.

Syracuse's last touchdown of the game was set up by a beautiful 49-yard run by a now-healthy Whitey Reimer, who turned and twisted his way down to the BU 15-yard line. Reserve back John Nichols ran it in on the next play. The final score was 46–0.

GERHARD SCHWEDES (Halfback): "We were leading 12–0 at the half, but Ben wouldn't even come in the locker room. Rocco Pirro came in, and Rock was the most gentle guy in the world. He sat down and said, 'Ben won't come in, he's mad at you guys, twelve points the first half.' So we went back out, and there was no way we were going to lose to that team. Ben called the offensive plays to me, and I gave them to Dave Sarette. After the first couple of sequences I just happened to look over to the BU bench and noticed that as soon as Ben gave me a signal, they gave a signal to their defense. Dumb German that I am, I put two and two together and I figured out those guys know our plays. We decided that Ben would keep calling the signals, but we're going to call our own plays in the huddle. So I told Sarette call what you want Dave, we're on our own. We just killed them in the second half; it was 46–0. What they had done, we found out later, was when we played Pittsburgh they had somebody there with a camera. They filmed both Ben and the game and they put two and two together. Ben gave the signal and they knew what was going to be called. It was clever, but it ultimately didn't work."

DAVE SARETTE (Quarterback): "I used to wear these big contacts. When I say big contacts, I mean Big Contacts. These use to fit under your eyelid, they weren't like today, where they fit over your pupils. I did have problems sometimes, especially if I got a finger in the eye, that would really irritate it. They would water up on me so many times that I had to take them out. Schwartzwalder would signal in the plays, and I never could see what he was signaling, he was too far away. I could see what was in front of me and stuff, I didn't have any problem that way, I just couldn't see him in the midst of the whole bench. I knew he's someplace there, I just couldn't see him. That's why Gerhard Schwedes used to always tell me what the play was."

MAURY YOUMANS (Tackle): "I do remember when we played Boston University in '59 a guy that was on that team, Peter Perrault, who went on to play with the Jets, and I believe the Giants, as a tackle. He reminded me that was the game that they named our whole line, 'Player Of The Week.' "

BU coach Steve Sinko praised Syracuse for being a "well-balanced team," who in his opinion had too much power for his team. Many of the BU players thought the Syracuse offense was the best they had ever played against, and quarterback Dave Sarette came in for praise for his ball-faking, which kept the BU defense confused at times.

Syracuse, for the ninth straight game, totally dominated the statistics. Syracuse rushed for 416 yards while holding BU to a minus 88 yards rushing. The Terriers did pass for 106 yards but were forced to punt eleven times compared to once by Syracuse. Listless in the first half, the players responded and now could get ready for a date with UCLA in two weeks at the Los Angeles Coliseum before a national audience on TV.

Al GERLICK

TACKLE

A writer for the local newspaper, Bill Clark, came down to the Slocum Hall dining room to interview me. He knew I was one of the few seniors on the second unit. He started asking me questions about the second unit, and I told him we were disappointed because the first unit naturally gets all the notoriety and we don't even barely get mentioned. We feel we're just as valuable. The first unit had the best personnel on offense, but we felt our defense was just as good or even a little better at times. The first unit had all these nicknames given to them like the 'Sizeable Seven' for the linemen, and the 'Four Furries' for the backs. I told him our group had nicknames, too. I just started rattling off nicknames, making some of them up as I went along, and not thinking anything of it. I went over all the nicknames like 'Cannonball' for myself, 'Rodent Stem,' 'Guts Neary,' and 'Sneaky Appelhof.' The next day Bill Clark writes this article about the second team's nicknames, including the ones I had made up. At practice guys were coming up to me saying, 'Cannonball, where did these nicknames come from?' Then to make matters worse, Red Smith, the syndicated columnist picked up the story, and it went national. So much for nicknames."

Al Gerlick. Courtesy of Syracuse University Athletic
Communications.

Roger Davis makes a tackle. Courtesy of Syracuse University Archives.

18

UCLA

Syracuse's biggest problem in preparation for UCLA was practicing outside because of the heavy snow that had fallen in Central New York. Ben Schwartzwalder was forced to work his team out in old Archbold gymnasium, as the University still lacked a field house in '59.

BEN SCHWARTZWALDER: "If we aren't able to get good conditions around here to practice we're going to be in trouble, in fact we're in trouble right now."

The situation was so bad that Ben was considering renting Colgate's field house and driving the thirty-nine miles down to Hamilton each day so his boys could get a good workout. UCLA, the Orange's opponent on the west coast, had no such problem as temperatures in Southern California were in the low eighties. The Bruins were looking forward to playing the nation's number one team, Two weeks before they had defeated Southern Cal, then ranked the number two team in the nation. All through the previous Saturday's easy win over Utah, the UCLA faithful were yelling, "Beat Syracuse!" It was going to be a big game for both teams. A crowd of 60,000 was expected at the Coliseum, along with millions watching on television across the country.

National recognition was coming to Syracuse players as Roger Davis and Fred Mautino were voted to the AP first team All America squad. Tackle/kicker Bob Yates and Roger Davis were named to Look Magazine's All America team and the Orangemen dominated the All East team, with five players being selected. Lineman Roger Davis, Bob Yates, and Fred Mautino were chosen along with running backs Art Baker and Gerhard Schwedes. Coach Ben Schwartzwalder was named Coach Of The Year by the Associated Press.

The Orangemen flew to California on the Thursday prior to the game to give the players one day to recuperate from the eleven hour flight. The team was scheduled to leave out of Hancock field at 9:30AM, but was forced to wait two extra hours as the plane taking them west got grounded in Columbus, Ohio due to fog. Schwartzwalder, still concerned about the lack of quality practice time in preparation for the Bruins, had scheduled a night practice at the Coliseum when the team landed in Los Angeles. Stopping once in Kansas City to take on food and fuel, the arrival in LA became extended. Because the airport was covered in a blanket of smog, the plane was rerouted to Burbank. Upon landing, much to the chagrin of Schwartzwalder, the team was met by a group of UCLA coeds passing out oranges and welcoming the team to sunny California. Schwartzwalder herded his troops into a waiting bus and quickly headed for the LA Coliseum and a night practice.

LEON CHOLOKIS (Tackle): "When we got to LA there was some serious smog. Ben had scheduled a practice and was not about to cancel it. I remember the trainers came around squeezing lemon juice in your throat so you would be able to breathe better. When Neil (Neil Pratt, Assistant Trainer) came over to squeeze it in my throat the cap came off and I swallowed the fucking cap. They didn't let me practice and brought me into the training room all nervous. After eleven hours in that prop plane, that was one practice I was happy to miss."

TOM GILBURG (End): "I remember we got out there and Ben had us practice in the Coliseum. There was a lot of smog, and Roy Simmons got laughing, he says,'Tom you're kicking the ball out of sight,' and I was."

VAL PINCHBACK (Syracuse Sports Information Director, 1959): "There was a guy named Fred Hilligis who was the news guy on WSYR during that time. He was a Cornell guy. Anyway, he thought he'd be cute on the end of the newscast and said, 'Incidentally, the

Leon Cholokis sacks Billy Kilmer. Courtesy of Syracuse University Archives.

rumor that the Syracuse team in Los Angeles has been hit by food poisoning is wrong, its false, that rumor is false.'

"Well of course there was no rumor: he started the rumor. I spent the whole day chasing that whole thing down because obviously there was no food poisoning. I went crazy the next day because I had to field a million phone calls. I mean you had all the newspapers calling, and I'm sure there were a few people probably betting a buck on the game, that wanted to know what was going on.

"The UCLA Bruins had won four games in a row coming into the Syracuse game. The coaching staff referred to them as 'The Fly Boys,' because of the tremendous speed and quickness they had throughout their lineup. Coach Bill Barnes, one of the last coaches left in college football to still run the Single Wing Offense, had a gifted passer in Bill Kilmer. Operating as the tailback, Kilmer was very adept at getting the ball to a trio of fine receivers led by Jim Johnson, the younger brother of decathlon champion Rafer Johnson. The last time the Orange had faced a Single Wing offense was the opening of the 1957 season against Iowa State, which ended in a 7–7 tie. The Bruins' hopes relied on being able to stop the penetration of Syracuse's big front lines. The Bruins would be giving up an average of 20 pounds a man along the line of scrimmage and hoped that their team's speed and quickness would offset the tremendous size differential. Also a concern for Bill Barnes was Syracuse's depth. Although he felt he could field two good teams against Syracuse, he questioned whether his team had the quality of reserves that the Orangemen had."

BILL BARNES (UCLA Head Coach): "We think its an honor to play a great team like Syracuse. They will know they have been in a ball game though. Our kids are dedicated, and if they can play the way they did against Southern Cal, we have a chance. This is a great challenge for us."

Bob Yates teed up the ball and, under Blue skies with the temperature 82 degrees, kicked off as he and his teammates attempted to become the first team in Syracuse football history to go undefeated and win a National Championship. Following the kickoff, UCLA went right to the air and on a series of short passes made a first down at their own 42-yard line. On first down, Bruin running back Ray Smith's pass down field was tipped by Gerhard Schwedes and intercepted by linebacker Al Bemiller, who returned the ball 12 yards before being tackled by Smith at the Bruin 44-yard line. On first down, rolling to his left, Syracuse quarterback Sarette found left end Skonieczki open on the sideline for a 11 yard completion. Coming back with an off tackle slant, Ernie Davis gained 10 yard. After three running plays moved the ball to the UCLA 6-yard line, Sarette, rolling out, found Schwedes wide open in the end zone for the touchdown. Bob Yates extra point made it 7–0.

After the kickoff UCLA ran two plays before taking a page out of Kansas's strategy and quick kicked. The ball traveled 50 yards and was downed with no return. Schwartzwalder, substituting his second unit, had reserve quarterback Dick Easterly run an option play on first down. Easterly, faking a pitch to halfback Mark Weber, kept the ball and ran around right end for 24 yards and a Syracuse first down just inside UCLA territory. On second down Easterly ran the same play, this time gaining 10 yards. Schwartzwalder, sensing UCLA was ripe for the "scissors play," signaled in to Easterly to call it. Taking the handoff, Easterly moved to the right, handing off to Halfback Mark Weber coming back left. Weber took the handoff and, seeing a gaping hole in the Bruin defense, sprinted 14 yards before being tripped up by defensive back, Jim Johnson. The Bruins called a time out and regrouped, holding Syracuse to 8 yards on three carries. Facing a fourth and two from the 15-yard line, Schwartzwalder decided to go for it. Easterly, rolling left, hit a wide open Weber in the end zone for the score. Al Gerlick's extra point made the score 14–0, with just over eleven minutes to go in the half.

Returning to the game, Syracuse's first unit stopped the Bruin offense cold on three straight plays, forcing UCLA to punt again. Gathering momentum after the punt Syracuse's first team pushed to midfield before Bruin Rod Cochren recovered a Davis fumble at the 50-yard line. UCLA quarterback Billy Kilmer, under a tremendous rush from the Syracuse front six, completed a series of short passes which moved the ball to the SU 18-yard line, but the drive was stopped on downs. After an exchange of punts, Schwartzwalder brought his second team back on the field. Behind the strong running of backs Bobby Hart and John Nichols, the second unit pushed down to the Bruin 1-yard line, where Easterly dove in for the score. Gerlick's kick made it 21–0.

Trailing by three scores and with only a couple minutes left before intermission, the Bruins put together their best drive of the day. Utilizing screen passes to negate the fierce Syracuse rush, UCLA marched quickly down the field, reaching the Syracuse 20-yard line. On a first and ten Kilmer spotted the speedy Jim Johnson behind the Syracuse secondary and hit him with a wobbly pass for the touchdown. Tailback Skip Smith ran it over for the two point conversion as the half ended. Syracuse lead at intermission, 21–8.

The third quarter found both teams unable to sustain any meaningful drives. Both teams turned the ball over, but neither team could capitalize on it. Syracuse's best opportunity was when Leon Cholokis and Roger Davis threw Kilmer for a loss, jarring the ball loose where Cholokis fell on it at midfield. A series of penalties by the Orange stopped that drive, and SU was forced to punt.

Finally, late in the third quarter, the Syracuse team was able to put together a drive. Starting from their own 19-yard line the Orange, off a Schwedes 40-yard run, moved deep into Bruin territory. Following a 10 yard gain up the middle by Ernie Davis, Schwedes scored off the "scissors play." The play, setup by some beautiful ball faking by the Sophomore quarterback Sarette, went for 23 yards. Sarette's completion to Tom Gilburg, subbing for the injured Fred Mautino, added two more points, stretching the lead to 29–8.

Knowing UCLA had to pass, Syracuse's second unit put tremendous pressure on the Bruin quarterback, sacking him twice in a row.

Left to right: Gerhard Schwedes, Dave Sarette, and Mark Weber celebrate UCLA win. Courtesy of Gerhard Schwedes.

Faced with a third and long Kilmer, under heavy pressure, threw wildly down field were Syracuse defender Ed Bowers intercepted the pass. The second team stayed in the game and marching down the field, ending in a Easterly pass to Mark Weber for the score. Appearing on national television, Syracuse's forgotten team, the second unit, had put on quite a show. The final score was 36–8. The Orangemen had run the table, a perfect 10–0. Only the Texas Longhorns stood in their way for an undisputed National Championship.

BILL BARNES (UCLA Head Coach): "As far as I'm concerned they're Number One. They're by far the best team we have played this year, and one of the greatest teams I've ever seen."

BEN SCHWARTZWALDER: "We of the decadent east are very happy with our win out west. We got hundreds of letters critizing us as not playing as tough a schedule as some other teams might have. I think this game answers those questions."

RAY SILLSET (Texas Coach/Scout): "Syracuse is the best team I have seen this year. If their not number one, I don't know who is."

AL WOLF (Writer, *LA Times*, 1959): "These Orangemen aren't human. I don't think I ever saw a tougher college team. Syracuse should have played the Rams."

PAUL ZIMMERMAN (Sports Editor, *LA Times*, 1959): "It has been a long time since such defensive strength and offensive poise have been seen in one college team on the Coliseum sod. We all knew we had seen one of college football's greatest teams."

MARK WEBER (Halfback): "A lot of people across the country didn't think we could stand up to these guys. Lindsey Nelson and Red Grange were doing the broadcast and I caught two touchdown passes from Dick Easterly. My Dad was taping the audio portion of the game and later on he played it back for me. He said, 'Listen to this.' Well Red Grange says, 'If Syracuse's first team is the Number One team in the country, then the second team must be Number Two.' I'll never forget that."

Syracuse again dominated the statistics as they had all year racking up 456 yards in total offense. UCLA was held to minus 13 yards rushing, but were able to pick up 160 yards through the air for a net total of 147 yards total offense for the game. Other than Fred Mautino who injured his ankle in the first quarter, Syracuse came through the game in good shape and was ready to return home to a welcoming like no other Syracuse team ever had.

Ernie Davis shows his skill in open field running. Courtesy of Gerhard Schwedes.

The Cotton Bowl

"Roger Davis and Gerhard were our captains for the Cotton Bowl game. When they went out for the coin toss before the game, the Texas band played 'The Eyes of Texas are Upon You.' When Roger came back to our sidelines he said, "Boys I think we are in for a ball game, when they played that song those guys had tears in their eyes."
—Maury Youmans

When the Number One Team in the nation arrived home following their win over UCLA, there was an estimated 10,000 people at Hancock field to greet them. Even the plane being two hours late didn't dampen the spirit of the excited fans, and thunderous cheers greeted the players, coaches and staff as the walked off the plane. The city of Syracuse had at that moment its greatest champion. Not since the Syracuse Nationals won the NBA title back in 1955 had this blue collar town had such pride. This was an even bigger event to the city because of the enormous interest in Syracuse football. A Cotton Bowl win over Texas would be the icing on the cake, but for now the town wanted to celebrate their National Champions.

Coach Ben Schwartzwalder, on the trip back, decided to give his players one week off before beginning practice in earnest for the Cotton Bowl.

BEN SCHWARTZWALDER: "The kids are going to have a week off to forget about football and catch up on their studies. Its been a long season, and they certainly have earned a break. We will start practice a week from today and I hope we can get outdoors, but I imagine the weather will be against us. We'll have four days of practice here, then we will leave for Houston. We will stay in Houston until December 30th, when we will go onto Dallas. When we're in Houston we'll practice twice a day, but we will take Sundays off."

After over three months of football the players would enjoy the time off, but that was not the case for the coaching staff who began developing a game plan for Texas. Ben Schwartzwalder was besieged by offers of personal appearances and speaking engagements. A trip to New York City to appear on the Ed Sullivan show turned into a nightmare because of the weather, and Ben barely got to the theater in time to be introduced by Sullivan. Also, rumors were flying that Boston of the new American Football League wanted Ben as there coach.

BEN SCHWARTZWALDER: "All I'm thinking about is getting ready for Texas. As far as I'm concerned, this is a ludicrous thing. Now I don't object to this sort of question being raised, but I don't have any ambitions to hunt for a job. I have no desire to leave Syracuse and I hope the folks in Syracuse like me. I'm not concerned if the folks in Boston do."

Media attention be damned, Ben wasn't going to lose focus on this upcoming game. . . . it was too important! He and the staff mapped out a schedule right through New Year's Day. Schwartzwalder, reflecting on the season, was glad that his team had a late game (Dec. 5th) against UCLA. In past seasons his teams would end the season in the middle of November, then have to wait six weeks before playing a Bowl game. He thought cutting that time in half this time around would be an advantage for his team. Schwartzwalder also was concerned about taking his three black players south. Ben didn't want to see any racial problems pop up. He made sure the facilities in Houston were setup for the entire team, as well as the hotel accommodations in Dallas. He wasn't going to stand for the black players having to stay somewhere else.

GERHARD SCHWEDES (Halfback): "When we went down for the Cotton Bowl, Ben wanted to avoid the black players having any racial problems. Being the captain, I was included in the meetings with the Athletic Director and the Chancellor to try to avoid our black players encountering any racial situations. They were very concerned about that."

Texas coach Darrell Royal, trying a different tactic, would conduct light drills through Christmas with no scrimmaging or hitting. He had overworked his team two years before in preparation for the Sugar Bowl, and his team had played poorly. He decided this time to cut back on his team's workload in getting ready for Syracuse.

Royal, like Ben Schwartzwalder, believed in hard-nosed football. He believed that you won football games by out hitting the opponent and wearing them down. His teams were described as 'Opportunistic', as they caused turnovers which many times led to victory. The Texas players had respect for the Orangemen after watching them on television dismantle a good UCLA team but issued a strong warning to the Syracuse players.

MAURICE DOKE (Texas All American Tackle): "We have all the respect for Syracuse. They are obviously a great team, but I honestly don't think they have been hit like were going to hit them."

Texas, like UCLA, had great team speed but also had good size along the front wall. Royal recruited tough kids, and under his leadership the Texas program was getting stronger each year. Offensively the Longhorns ran what Royal described as a 'Conglomerate T Formation.' Royal, when asked to describe it said, "If there's a definite trend in college regarding offense, we aren't following it." The Longhorns well balanced attack featured two speedy backs, Jack Collins and Rene Ramierz. Both halfbacks were adept passers who were given ample opportunities to throw the ball. Up front Texas had an outstanding line led by Maurice Dokes and right tackle Larry Stephens. The battle up front between two very good lines would probably determine the outcome of the game.

When Syracuse arrived in Houston on December 19th, everyone was pleased with the facilities. The practice field, the living quarters and, most importantly to the players, the weather was nice. The Orangemen settled in and had ten days of good practices before heading for Dallas and a date with Texas in the Cotton Bowl .

The 1960 Cotton Bowl was the most anticipated of all the major bowls that year because of the match up of two great teams. Syracuse, the only undefeated team left in the country, had one more hill to climb. . . . beating the Texas Longhorns! Syracuse, with its past history of never winning a Bowl game, was still considered a 'Paper Champion,' by much of the country, and until it could beat a top-ranked team like the Longhorns, that attitude would continue. Mississippi and LSU, ranked second and third in the final polls, would square off again in the Sugar Bowl, with the winner of that game probably winning the National Championship if Syracuse lost to Texas. The Longhorns hoped a solid win over the Number One team in the nation might catapult the Texans right past the two teams above them, Mississippi and LSU, and give them the National Championship. The pressure to win the title, and finally put to rest the belief that Eastern football was inferior to the rest of the country, was squarely on the shoulders of the Syracuse team.

Three days prior to the Cotton Bowl game Ernie Davis was out early for practice, which was a normal routine for him. Davis, who had been the place kicker on his high school team, was impressing the few players out on the field with his kicking abilities. Attempting a 50 yard field goal, Ernie felt a twinge in his thigh, followed by some excruciating pain. Falling to the ground holding his thigh the young player knew he had done something stupid; he may have jeopardized his chance to play in the biggest game of his life. Syracuse Head Trainer Julie Reichel helped Davis back to the locker room, where they iced down the thigh and began treatment to try to get their star player healthy enough to play. The chances of doing that in three days were slim. A worried Ben Schwartzwalder went on with practice with one eye looking toward the locker room; this foolish accident was not good.

A capacity crowd of 75,204 fans crammed the Cotton Bowl to

watch the first meeting between Syracuse and Texas. In the Syracuse locker room Julie Reichel was fitting Ernie Davis with a pair of long johns to hopefully add more support to his strained thigh. Reichel and his staff had scoured the Dallas area the day before trying to find this underwear garment for the injured Davis to wear. Ernie was determined to play and would not take no for an answer. The training staff knew he was in tremendous pain but were not going to stop him from trying. They doubted he could last more than a few plays. He was one tough guy.

Syracuse won the toss and elected to receive. Dropping back deep for the Orangemen were Gerhard Schwedes and Whitey Reimer, who was replacing Ernie Davis on the kickoff. The Longhorn's kick was fielded by Schwedes at the 5-yard line. Breaking to his left the Syracuse Captain returned the kickoff to the Syracuse 29-yard line. On first down Texas tackle Maurice Doak smacked Art Baker behind the line of scrimmage for a one yard loss. On second down Sarette rolled left, over-throwing Jerry Skonieczki who was open at the Syracuse 40-yard line, but there was a flag on the field. Syracuse was penalized for holding, pushing the ball back to the Syracuse 13-yard line. The Orange had stumbled out of the gate; they were definitely feeling the pressure. It was now second down and 26 yards to go for a first down. The Texas players were pumped! They were out hitting their opponents, and in their minds the Syracuse players looked scared. The Orangemen came out of the huddle unbalanced to the right, Ernie Davis was split to the left side. Sarette, taking the snap from center Al Bemiller, quick pitched to Schwedes who was running right on a apparent power sweep. Schwedes, taking the pitch, dropped back and looked down field looking for his receivers. Initially seeing Skonieczki covered, he looked for Ernie Davis but couldn't find him. Now feeling the pressure from the Texas defense, Schwedes continued rolling right looking, looking for Davis but not finding him. As the Syracuse captain came near the sidelines, he threw the ball deep and high in the air hoping Davis would be there. Seemingly out of nowhere appeared 'number 44', running as hard as he could, separating himself from the Texas defenders. Davis caught the ball in mid stride and set sail for the Texas goal line. Noticeably limping, this great athlete was not going to be caught, running 87 yards for a touchdown . . . a new Cotton Bowl record! The Longhorns were stunned., Syracuse had struck first; this time around the Orangemen were ready to play.

GERHARD SCHWEDES (Halfback): "The first pass to Ernie Davis in the Cotton Bowl wasn't planned because we had to pass, it was third and twenty-six. Ben had a lot of confidence in me throwing; he had a lot of confidence in all his halfbacks throwing the ball. I had the option of Running or throwing on that play, but first I had to sell the run. The defense initially had to think we were running the ball to give the receivers an opportunity to get open. Ernie, on that play, ran the wrong route. It was supposed to be a sideline pass. Jerry Skoniecki was supposed to be fifteen yards down the field on the sideline, far enough to get the first down. Ernie was then supposed to be another eight to fifteen yards in back of him, also a sideline pattern. In Ben's option pass, both guys are supposed to be in the halfback's line of vision . . . one player 15 yards down field, the other player 25 yards down field. I looked first at Skoniezcki; he was covered and double teamed. Ernie was no where in sight. What he did, instead of running sideline pattern, he ran a post pattern. He just took off down field. I heaved it as far as I could, and he ran under it."

Texas returned the Syracuse kickoff back to their 40-yard line and received an additional 15 yards on a holding penalty called on the Orangemen. The Longhorns gained 2 yards on first down. Then, after an incomplete pass, running back Jack Collins was stopped one foot short of the first down. Texas, now on the Syracuse 36-yard line, decided to go for it. Trying to run wide, the pitch back to halfback Bobby Gurwitz sailed over his head, and Syracuse defender Skonieczki recovered the errant pitch on Texas's 48-yard line. The Texas defense stiffened, and Syracuse was forced to punt. Both teams were unable to move the ball and continued to trade punts through the remainder of the first quarter.

Midway through the second quarter the Orangemen began a drive from their own 20-yard line. On first down, off the scissors play, Ernie Davis ran for 19 yards. A series of bootlegs by Sarette off the Syracuse ride series netted another 15 yards. Two passes, one to Fred Mautino and another Schwedes to Skonieczki, placed the ball at the Texas 1-

Mark Weber tackles a Texan. Courtesy of Syracuse University Archives.

yard line. On first down Sarette dove for the touchdown but was ruled short of the goal line by the referee. On second down Sarette scored again but was ruled short of the goal line. Ben Schwartzwalder was livid! All game Syracuse was getting calls he felt were improper. From his vantage point his quarterback had clearly scored twice. On third down Ernie Davis slid off tackle into the end zone for the score. Syracuse went for two, and Sarette hit Davis for the two-point conversion. Syracuse led 15–0.

The game became very physical as both teams continued to pound each other. Late in the second period it came to a head. Tackles John Brown for Syracuse and Longhorn Larry Stephens grabbed each other following a play. Brown, one of three Blacks on the team, had, according to his teammates, been constantly called "Nigger" throughout the game by Stephens. Players from both teams ran on the field and a melee erupted. The emotion of the game had created an ugly scene. Coaches from both sides tried to calm their players down. Finally peace was restored, and the game continued with no more scoring in the first half.

Starting the third period Texas scored quickly. Facing a third and twelve from their own 31-yard line, Texas quarterback Bob Lackey faked a jump pass and dropped back and spotted Jack Collins wide open down field. Lackey's pass was perfect, and Collins ran untouched into the end zone for the Longhorns' first score. Trailing now 15–6,

Texas attempt for two points failed when Ernie Davis came up from his defensive back position and tackled Collins running wide at the 5-yard line.

Syracuse marched back down the field reaching the Texas 23-yard line, but a Sarette pass to the end zone was intercepted by the Longhorns' Mike Cotten. Three plays later Cotten had the tables turned on him. The Texas backup quarterback, under pressure from Roger Davis, threw down field where Ernie Davis intercepted the ball at the Texas 36-yard line. . . . returning it 12 yards to give his team great field position at the Texas 24. On second down Davis ran right, looking to pass, but could not find anyone open. Now, running left and reversing field, he picked up a wall of blockers and motored down to the 3-yard line before being knocked out of bounds. On first down Schwedes burst off right guard for the touchdown. Sarette's easy flip to Davis in the end zone added another two points, stretching the Syracuse lead to 23–6.

The two teams continued to battle as the third period wound down. Syracuse, with their second unit in the game, turned the ball over to Texas on a Dick Easterly fumble. Starting from the Syracuse 34-yard line, two Bobby Lackey passes to Rene Ramierz moved the ball to the Syracuse 4-yard line. Texas had first and goal. The Syracuse defense was once again called upon to hold the line. On three running plays Texas moved to the Oranges' 1-yard line, but on fourth down the big front wall of Syracuse stopped Texas at the six inch line and SU took over on downs.

The Longhorns continued to play hard, forcing Syracuse to punt. Getting the ball back, this time Texas found the end zone on a six play drive which saw Lackey dive over from the 3-yard line. His two point conversion to Schultz put the score at 23–14.

Neither team could move the ball as the game approached its final minutes. Texas, facing a fourth down deep in their own territory, was forced to punt. Ernie Davis, back deep to receive the kick, decided not to risk a fumble and let the ball roll. Unfortunately his teammate Ed Bowers wasn't thinking like Ernie and reached for the ball as two Texas players converged on him, causing a fumble. Texas recovered at the Syracuse 29. Desperately trying to score, four passes by Lackey fell short as the clock ran out.

Gerhard and Ben accepting the Cotton Bowl Trophy. Courtesy of
Syracuse University Archives.

Syracuse had won its first National Championship in perhaps the
most physical and at times dirty football game ever witnessed in the
Cotton Bowl. This classic contest between two great teams would be
marred with racial overtones and questionable officiating. *Life* magazine, which was there to do a piece nominating Syracuse as the best
team of the decade, decided to change the story line because of the
fight between the teams. Both coaches, visibly concerned about the
fight, tried to focus on the hard fought game.

DARRELL ROYAL (Texas Head Coach): "I've never been
prouder; the kids got after them good. I don't think Syracuse was lucky
to win, but I think we could have won. It was a great effort, as good as
you can get. Our Texans are competitors. They had several chances to
fold, but you saw they didn't."

BEN SCHWARTZWALDER: "This is a real fine football team,
the best we faced this year, but we pretty much knew this in advance.

Texas has a good balance of speed and balance, and Darrel Royal is a real fine coach."

BOBBY LACKEY (Texas Quarterback): "I'd say they are a very fine team, the best team we have faced this year, but I think were pretty good too."

MAURICE DOKES (Texas All American Tackle): "Roger Davis is a real fine boy and a real All American. It was a pleasure to play against such a good team. I'd love to play against them again next week. Yes, they are better than TCU or Arkansas."

The Syracuse players were upset about the treatment of John Brown, and many thought the Texas players went over the line with dirty play. Larry Stephens defended himself saying he didn't say anything racial. John Brown took the high road and said it was just a tough game.

Ernie Davis was awarded the Most Valuable Trophy award for his play. The Young sophomore played in tremendous pain and all of America that watched that day saw what a great player he was. Davis was to receive his award at the Cotton Bowl Dinner that evening.

The next day Gerhard Schwedes and Bob Yates got married in Dallas. The Syracuse players had a fitting celebration to a most improbable year, finishing undefeated and Number One in the nation.

DAVE APPELHOF (Center): "It was a bittersweet experience. I thought the game was outstanding, but I know as the game wore on it no longer became a football game . . . it became a battle. In that sense you knew you were up there to protect yourself. You're out there to win the game, but it changed from a college competitive sport to one of a vicious battle. I got hit, I got blind sided harder in that game that in my mind should have been a clip. I stayed in the game, I actually played a couple of plays; then when we went out I was on the bench and I basically came to. It was a really strange feeling."

JOHN BROWN (Tackle): "We were in Dallas and we were staying at the Monroe Hotel and we were behind the kitchen. We were on the first floor. We were instructed to stay off the elevators. That didn't bother me, because those were the times. One player that was staying in the room with us, I'll never forget it, said his Mom and Dad were in town or some kind of bullshit and it was nothing against us, but he couldn't stay with us. Mike Neary came up and said, "I don't give a damn where I stay, I'll stay with you guys." I'll never forget that. Mike was a super guy and I'll never forget that. He just took his stuff and switched rooms with this individual. He just came down there and he just fitted in with, at that time it was me, Art (Baker) and Ernie (Davis)."

BOB YATES (Tackle): "I remember the game very vividly, but the riot and the fights and all of that stuff that broke out . . . it kind of soured me. What is really great is that I'm down here in Texas, and ninety percent of the people down here are University of Texas people. I bring up quite often about Syracuse kicking the hell out of Texas in the Cotton Bowl. They're not too happy about that, but that's the way it goes. They'll never get over it down here. Texas people, they got a memory that is longer than a football field, they know and they remember."

John BROWN

TACKLE

I look at it now, and of course I'm sixty-five, it was the times and I was brought up in one area, he was brought up in another. That was his thing. Today now he's probably one of the best gentlemen around. (Larry Stephens is deceased.) We were fighting to win. Today you called me those names, you said those things to me I would probably laugh at you and walk away. I was eighteen, nineteen at the time. I'm from Camden, New Jersey, and we're fighting to win, we're doing everything we can do to win. The name calling had no place on the field. I was in Dallas two years ago, to Ernie's induction into the Cotton Ball Hall of Fame. Darryl Royal (Texas coach) came up and he apologized to me, he really did. I said, 'Coach, that's alright, that was the times.' but he says, 'Hey, I had no idea what was being said on the field.' You know he didn't have to come over and apologize to me. He never had the opportunity to confront either me, Ernie, or Art Baker."

Gerlick, Grabowski, and Brown sacking the quarterback. Courtesy of Al Gerlick.

Ernie Davis. Courtesy of Syracuse University Sports Information.

20

Ernie Davis

"When you talk about Ernie Davis, you're treading on hallowed ground. We always thought he had a halo around him, and now we know he has."
—Ben Schwartzwalder

When discussing Ernie Davis to the people who knew him one thing comes out every time: This man was loved and respected. His impact on the '59 team is immeasurable and the profound emotion that exudes at the mere mention of his name forty-four years later is extraordinary. Ernie transcended the qualities of what good people are all about. He wasn't just an All-American football player, he was an All-American human being. He stood for what's good in people, he stood for what's good in athletics, he stood for what's good about caring for others and being a friend. In the unjust world that he lived in during the 1960s, he marched forward, never bitter, always friendly, enjoying people probably as much as they enjoyed him. He loved children and they loved him. He was a comet in our horizon, gone before we knew it. There's a picture of him at his high school, Elmira Free Academy, with the inscription, "He could do it all, beat every opponent . . . except one." I believe that sums it up.

ERNIE DAVIS (Halfback, six weeks before he died, explaining in

Ernie Davis accepting Cotton Bowl MVP award as Lou Andreas (far left) looks on. Courtesy of Syracuse University Archives.

the *Saturday Evening Post* his feelings about playing football): "A lot of things go into it, the excitement, the physical contact, the skill, the crowds, but the big thing to me in football has always been the competitiveness. Sometimes, when the game is close and the play is the roughest, you forget the crowd and the noise. It's just you against somebody else to see who is the better man. This is what I liked and took pride in."

JOHN BROWN (Tackle): "Ernie was an exceptional person, he really was. He was like a brother to me. His mom is my son's godmother: that's how close we got. My senior year I roomed with Pete Brokaw, and John Mackey and Ernie roomed side by side to us. We all kind of hung out together. I'm from Camden, New Jersey, and one holiday I was having a party at my house. Forty black students at Syracuse at that time all went down to my house. Ernie had an exam so I had to wait for him because he didn't know how to get to Camden, New Jersey. He had an Edsel, and I'll never forget we were on our way down to Camden and the car broke down in a place called Carbondale, PA. It was a little mill town, one hotel, one movie theater. I think we spent five hours seeing Moby Dick, over and over and over again, which drove me crazy. The garage had to send to Philadelphia for the part. I'm calling down to my house and everybody is having a good time at *my* party. Ernie and I are sitting in Carbondale,

"Number 44" on the loose in Archbold Stadium. Courtesy of Syracuse
University Archives.

PA, trying to get down there. By the time we got there the party was
over."

JOE SZOMBATHY (Assistant Coach): "Ernie was the only black
player on the Syracuse 1958 freshmen team. The freshmen coach was
Les Dye, and the first day he gathered the players around and said,
'Boys, we got Ernie Davis here. He comes to us with a lot of creden-
tials. Ernie says he's going to be a leader.' Les Dye looks at Ernie and
says, 'Ernie, now you go out there in front and lead the team in calis-
thenics.' And man did he lead them! He had them doing all kinds of
stretches, some very tough ones, but he was smiling and laughing all
through them. He gained everybody's respect right away."

DAN RACKIEWICZ (Linebacker): "Ernie caught a punt and he
was running it back and Mike Neary just blind-sided him, just absolutely creamed him. I thought Schwartzwalder was going to have a
heart attack. I mean, he chewed Neary out so much for a good hit that
you couldn't believe it. I mean he was really protecting his boy then.
He knew Ernie was really going to be something."

BILL RAPP, JR. (Student Manager): "When Ernie was a freshman I remember him in a punting drill. It was supposed to be full con-

tact. A couple of the varsity guys covering the punt said, 'We're going to test this kid.' So he caught the punt, this is the preseason, and these guys are bearing down on him, and they meant business, they wanted to hit him hard. Ernie got the ball and he squared up and they hit him simultaneously, one on the right shoulder, one on the left shoulder. He went right through the both of them. Both guys ended up on their butts and Ernie just jogged up the field. Backfield coach Bill Bell was standing there and he looks over at me and he goes, 'He's pretty coachable.' "

JIM SHREVE (Freshmen Coach): "I remember Ernie coming to my house when my kids were real small and I still have the autographed football he signed. We had gone to a Boy Scout meeting in Fayetteville. My kids were in elementary school and he came to our house and he went in the kids' room and talked to them. He was just a tremendous guy, he was so talented and so humble. I mean, I don't ever remember playing, or coaching, or being associated with anybody who was so humble and quiet, just a gentleman. The only guys that were close to him in ability, who I coached, were Floyd Little and Larry Csonka. Ernie was a straight-line runner but he still had some shiftiness in him. Ernie was more of a power-runner like Jim Brown, but still he had the ability to change directions. He was great. I'll tell you the thing about Ernie that is interesting, he ran tailback in the right-formation, and wingback in the left-formation. He had to learn both positions. How many tailbacks become wingbacks today? Not many."

DAVE SARETTE (Quarterback): "Ernie Davis babysat my two boys so my wife and I could go out. What a saint this guy was. He was a terrific person."

MAURY YOUMANS (Tackle): "Ernie was an exceptional individual. Ernie not only could play football, he got along well with people. He would win over the hearts of people immediately when you met him. When he was sick he also showed what a high caliber individual he was. I remember coming back that year to spring practice. I came up behind Ernie and grabbed him by the arm. My hands just went through his muscle. I thought at the time, 'Wow, this is not good.' He and I were not playing in that spring game so we had our

Ernie speaks while Ben doodles plays. Courtesy of Syracuse University Archives.

pictures taken along the sidelines. That was the last picture taken of him before his death a few weeks later. That picture ended up as a national picture of Ernie the day after he died."

BOB YATES (Tackle): "Ernie Davis was probably the best football player I ever played with. He was a great man, a great player. I just loved the guy, he was just a super football player."

DAVE BAKER (End): "He was one of the nicest guys I ever met.

I remember going back there when they unveiled the portrait of him at one of the spring football games. I cried when they unveiled that portrait of him."

GERHARD SCHWEDES (Halfback): "Ernie was one of the gentlest, nicest guys I have ever met in my whole life. He was just a great kid. He did everything he was supposed to do."

DAVE APPELHOF (Center): "Ernie Davis is just an outstanding individual, just a class guy all the way around, probably as classy a guy as I've met since I've been alive."

JOHN BROWN (Tackle): "You will never hear a bad thing about Ernie, you never will. HBO and some of the movie producers over the years have contacted me to write a movie about Ernie. I have interviewed with four, five, six of those writers. The one thing they always come up with is, they were never able to make a movie because they couldn't find anything controversial about him. Isn't it a sad commentary that you can't make a movie, or didn't want to make a movie, because you can't put a little something in there to make people want to see the dirt?"

BILL BELL (Assistant Coach): "Ernie Davis was such a dedicated person, really a very humble person. He would come in the office every day and you could just sit down and talk to him. You always knew where you stood with Ernie. He just had that sixth sense that great running backs have, good balance. He had speed, he could catch the ball, and he had the size.

"Ernie came in one day and he had a hat that was given to him that was expressly made for Ernie Davis. He gave it to me and I really valued that hat. Damned if someone didn't steal it."

JIM ANDERSON (Halfback): "Ernie I loved. I mean, that is still the saddest moment when he died. I got a little story about him. Of course we all have them. When we went back for the alumni game in '63, he's standing there in a nice suit and looked super, but he's sweating. I'm kind of shy so I don't say anything but Ernie just took over the situation, telling me about practicing in the pros and this and that. Two or three weeks later he died. That was sad. What a great guy. I don't want to get into it but what a super individual he was."

JOE SZOMBATHY (Assistant Coach): "Every summer we would

go to a coaches' clinic in Canton, Ohio. Ben had coached there before the war and liked to go back there each year and see old friends. It was while we were at the clinic that the news came out that Ernie had a blood disorder and was in the hospital. So after the clinic we drove over to see him. Well, we couldn't believe what the hell he looked like in the few short months since he left school. He was bloated, pasty looking, but that great attitude was there. He just said, 'I'll get over this.' "

GERHARD SCHWEDES (Halfback): "My first wife was from Elmira and her mother helped arrange Ernie's funeral at her church because it would hold ten thousand people. It was unbelievable the turnout for Ernie's funeral. The players and coaches from Syracuse, the Cleveland Browns team. He never got to play for the Cleveland Browns, but thirty of them showed up. It was a hard day with some of his family members attacking the casket, so emotionally spent. They couldn't let him go. He was a wonderful human being."

The Coach. Courtesy of Syracuse University Archives.

21

The Many Sides of Ben Schwartzwalder

The 'absent-minded professor of football' at Syracuse in 1959 was legendary for his complete dedication to the game of football. Ben Schwartzwalder found out early what he wanted to do with his life and followed that path until he retired in 1973. Those who worked with him, worked for him, and the players that played on his teams all have interesting stories to tell. Highly competitive, basically a shy man, the public never got to know the real Floyd Burdette Schwartzwalder in the same way his football family did.

Playing Golf

BILL BELL (Assistant Coach): "The best thing that ever happened to us as assistant coaches was when Ben started playing golf because up until he played golf we were in that office all the time. It was football, football, twelve months a year. But once he started playing golf he kind of loosened up and we had a little more leeway then. His handicap was always what he wanted it to be. He was very tough to beat on a golf course because of that changing handicap."

"27 HANDICAP?" Courtesy of Syracuse University Archives.

VAL PINCHBACK (Syracuse Sports Information Director, 1959): "You couldn't beat Benny playing golf because you never knew which ball he was counting. He'd say, 'That's my real one.'"

"We entered with our wives a 'Husband and Wife Golf Tournament' one time at Drumlins. With Benny's handicap, whatever the hell it was, we won about every hole. The next time they had a 'Husband and Wife Tournament,' the people there weren't anxious to have us play. I decided I didn't want to get involved in any more club tournaments with him and have the same people pointing their fingers at me.

I wasn't the bad guy here, Benny was, so I stopped playing tournaments with him."

MAURY YOUMANS (Tackle): "One time we won a golf tournament in Syracuse. It was the Syracuse Alumni Tournament. I was playing with Ben and when they announced the winner, everybody booed. All the alumni booed us. They knew it was impossible to beat Ben because of his floating handicap. But he would defend his floating handicap. He would tell me, 'I go to these coaches' conventions and they all cheat. I need to be prepared because they all cheat.' "

IDA PIRRO: "Ben, Rock, Ted, and I believe Joe Szombathy was the fourth, used to play in a 'Father and Child's Open' up in Pompey. They played for two or three years and won it each year. They won because Ben was carrying a twenty-five handicap. They finally barred them from playing in the tournament. Ben played everyday at Drumlins in the summer but he never posted his score. He just played by himself. He was shooting in the seventies but he carried a twenty-five handicap. He was a sandbagger."

The Head Coach

AL BEMILLER (Center): "Ben and I never saw eye-to-eye. One time, which I didn't like, he said that I would never make the freshman football team because I wasn't tough enough. That sort of hurt me. Funny thing was I never had much to do with him. I dealt mainly with the line coaches Ted Dailey and Rocco Pirro, but he was a great coach, he knew how to maneuver people around. I respected him for his coaching."

MARK WEBER (Halfback): "Ben was tough, no doubt about it. He put me down a number of times when I thought I should be playing more. On one hand he was tough but on the other he was sure a great influence on me later on. It's the old story, 'Boy, there's always someone a little bigger, a little stronger, so have respect for your opponent.' That's something I always remembered."

DAVE BAKER (End): "Ben Schwartzwalder was a good psychologist. He would say after a game, 'Okay, now you did good, now we got another game coming up,' and then he would talk it over very calmly. Always with his pipe in his mouth, and then he said, 'Now this is Saturday night. I want you to go out and have a good time but remember, we have practice Monday.' He was a very practical guy."

TOM GILBURG (End): "Ben was the greatest doctor I ever met. One time I had a root canal done and I didn't think I could practice. I went to Ben and I said, 'Coach I had a root canal done this morning' and before I could finish, Ben says, 'That's good, Tom, I'll see you at practice.'"

DAN RACKIEWICZ (Linebacker): "I remember one story that really stuck with me all my life, it was my sophomore year and I had to see my academic advisor. I made an appointment which made me miss practice. Schwartzwalder said, 'Dan, that's not the thing to do. You can find other times of the day to see your adviser. Don't ever miss practice again.' So the next year I thought he'll never remember that and I did it a second time. He called me into his office and said, 'I'm telling you, don't ever do that again or you're off the team.' He meant it. I didn't think he would remember, but he did. Needless to say, I didn't miss practice again and I learned a valuable lesson—when someone tells you something like that, you better listen."

X's and O's, . . . Chalkboards, . . . Stale Coffee

JOE SZOMBATHY (Assistant Coach): "Ben was just a fanatic on the chalkboard. He'd get up on that chalkboard. He loved to use the chalk. He would want to diagram plays and make little changes all the time. At the beginning of meetings he would say, 'Look, you know, I was thinking about this overnight, and we can do this, you know, and we can do that.' That carried on throughout all of his coaching days. He would just love to get up there and maybe review blocking assignments or put in new plays. He was always experimenting. We would have fade blocks and cross blocks, isolations, and traps. He was always dickering. He just loved to get on that board and he would listen to the other guys, but ultimately, it was his decision on most everything."

DICK EASTERLY (Quarterback): "During games I wished Ben would have stayed at one end of the bench to be perfectly honest. Don't get me wrong, he was a great coach. He gets you up and he controlled the game. But sometimes he would get a little excited when things didn't go his way. The reason I mention staying at the end of the bench is because I had to stand next to him all the time as a quarterback. It would be either myself or Dave Sarette. We usually didn't wear any rib protectors, but quarterbacks at Syracuse usually had to, because if you stood next to Ben he would hit you in the ribs constantly when the other guy did something wrong."

MAURY YOUMANS (Tackle): "Ben's life was football. I remember if we went to a banquet or lunches I hated to sit next to him. You tried to avoid the seat next to him. All he would do was sit there and draw plays. His mind was always 100 percent either on designing plays or getting plays ready for the next game."

DAVE SARETTE (Quarterback): "I coached for ten years afterwards and had a lot of success with the unbalanced line. It is a power offense. If you can get somebody to run the ride series well, to put that ball in the stomach and draw people in, there is a lot of flexibility to it. I liked having a short side because you can get out there quick and see your receivers. You can see what is going on very quickly without a lot of people in your way. I think I threw to my left ends more than I threw to anybody.

"The reason you don't see other coaches using the unbalanced line is because no one understands it. The core group of Ben's coaches stayed with him their entire careers so the knowledge of the running of that unbalanced line stayed right in Syracuse. Even though people were able to watch it they weren't able to understand it. There was a lot to understand, and I was fortunate to run it for those three years. I understood it very well, I still know it very well. Take for instance the option that people run today. Schwartzwalder was running that option in 1959. Ben was the first coach to make the belly option popular, and because he won, everybody started to notice. Look at that belly option and how well that works. The Oklahoma team in the 1959 Orange Bowl came with the option. They called it a 'split-T option.'

"The most famous play of all is the '74 scissors.' You have to run the ride series to make those scissors plays work. The scissors was just a misdirection play that came off real quick. It wasn't a trap, it was just straight blocking that took the momentum of the team going for the ride in one direction, then wham, you were coming back the other way. The linemen took their man where ever they wanted to go because of that type of blocking. The back would hit sometimes the hole inside or sometimes wide. Wherever the hole was he would hit, but he was hitting it quick."

BEANO COOK (ESPN Football Commentator): "The Syracuse coaches dressed like coaches. All these other coaches dress like their modeling for Brooks Brothers, with fancy ties and coats. The Syracuse coaches . . . looked like football coaches."

Ben and Friends

VAL PINCHBACK (Syracuse Sports Information Director, 1959): "When I was first at Syracuse as Sports Information Director, I was twenty-five years old. I began playing golf out at Drumlins where Benny belonged and the next thing you know we started spending a lot of time together socially. Our friendship, spending time together, helped me out professionally as I could walk into any meeting they had on anything and was accepted."

GERHARD SCHWEDES (Halfback): "My freshman year he called me aside and he said, 'You got the same clothes on all the time. Do you need help with clothes?' I said, 'no I'm fine,' but he said, 'Look, I know this guy downtown, I want you to go see him.' So he sent me downtown to this store. I got a half a dozen pair of underwear and some sport coats which I'd never had before. He fitted me for some dress pants, shoes, and whatever else I needed. Ben knew who was hurting and who wasn't, and he took care of people who were."

DAVE SARETTE (Quarterback): "I loved Rocco Pirro and Ted Dailey, I just thought the world of Roy Simmons but my favorite coach was Ben Schwartzwalder. He and his wife Reggie were always there for the married guys. They were very concerned people and they showed it often. Reggie Schwartzwalder would call my wife and see how she was, and she always asked about our two kids. It was little things like that. Schwartzwalder was more of a sensitive guy than most people think. If you played for him he was good by you. That's what he required."

A Poet

Ben and Reggie celebrated their fiftieth wedding anniversary in 1983 with many of their friends from Syracuse. After the dinner, Ben stood up and recited the following poem:

Ben and Reggie—Fiftieth Wedding Anniversary

Alphabetically seated in every class,
Got me acquainted with this fair lass.
In Morgantown W. Va. At W.V.U.,
We spent four years and then we were thru.
Not with each other just W.V.U.
I finally convinced her I was ok,
So she acquiesced to let me stay.
March 16th was the day we found,
Both the minister and I could be around.
The luckiest day of all my life,
Fifty years ago Reggie became my wife.
Weston and Sistersville soon slid by,
In Parkersberg we were mighty spry.
As State Champs with great kids came,
Now one of our own, Susan by name.
Canton was next, a one year stand,
Mary joined in, we brought out the band.
February 2nd of '42, gave us another thing to do.
Uncle Sam let it be known, he wanted me in as one of his own.
 Never a plane had I been in,
Not too smart, I proved again.
As football fans had often told,
All I needed, just the bold.
To jump out of planes with a gun,
From Georgia to Nebraska was supposedly fun.
Reggie went with me, along with the girls,
It proved conclusively I had three pearls.
Training we did, for we were at war,

Tough as it was, it wasn't a bore.
By the fall of '43, we were in England, over the sea.
D-Day came the 6th of June,
In Normandy we jumped soon.
For forty-three days we stayed and fought,
We did the things that we were taught.
The Bulge was next, for sixty-eight days,
Zero weather and Germans, we needed a blaze.
Then across the Rhine and into Munster,
Even this was no funster.
When the Germans gave up, on the Essen,
As Military Governor, I had their blessen'.
I was one of them, they tried to say,
I remember Normandy, I said "nay."
We hurried back home, fast as we could,
Fate would decree, it turned out good.
We'd been to Muhlenberg, to check the score,
About coaching football, nothing more.
Now, could I coach basketball as well?
If I couldn't, I wouldn't tell.
So I said yes, Why not?
It wouldn't do to ruin the plot.
To the NIT finals in N.Y. we did go,
Everyone said it was quite a show.
As basketball coach, it was my end.
On football now, my time I did spend.
We recruited key players, not bloopers,
From Parkersburg, Canton and my paratroopers.
A Tobacco Bowl win over St. Bonaventure,
Was truly more than a casual adventure.
Our three-year record was 25–5,
Lew Andreas now called me quite a surprise.
We studied our films and made calls.
To all of our opponents of the past three falls.
They said we were good and really hit,
Lou was impressed, he thought I would fit.

At Syracuse, it was our fate,
Almost an obsession, "Beat Colgate!"
From '49 throught '73, 25 years,
A lot of joy, a bit of tears.
By now I knew why I loved to coach,
So many kids beyond reproach.
An education was there with work,
They knew the price, they dare not shirk.
Our schedule got tougher, we need to grow,
Alabama creamed us in the Orange Bowl.
At least we got there, now we knew,
We needed more players, we had too few.
Two bowl games later, now '59,
We were ready to really shine.
We'd gone to the coast and whipped UCLA,
Their press had said we couldn't play.
The Civil War could've been tame,
Compared to Texas and the Cotton Bowl game.
They used every trick known to man and beast,
It was our day to have the feast.
23–14 the final score,
With other officials, it could have been more.
National Champions at long last,
In the spotlight we did bask.
Coach of the Year, Pres. Of the Coaches Assn,
It pleased the fans, it gave relations.
I'm dragging this out, better cut down,
Friends and family are all around.
Daughters we had, a very good start,
Sons came along, by way of the heart.
Walker and Scofield, now part of the clan,
Neither could wish for a better man.
Even tho they shortened their name,
They did so well, there is no blame.
Felicia, Brian, Libby are the Walker's three,
A wonderful addition as you can see.

Susan and Drew, the Scofield two,
Couldn't be here because of school.
Now my Pine Grove song for the Simpson clan,
On Simpson Hill they made a stand.
Get 'er ready, let 'er rip,
Get your composure, take a sip.
I'll sing the first verse, then you can join in,
We'll all then be real close kin.
And into the future, don't let it end!

With that we all sang our alma mater.

Celebrating Reggie's eightieth birthday, Ben took pencil in hand and wrote:

To Reggie My Lady Who Is 80

We met when Reggie was seventeen,
She had auburn hair and eyes of green.
A sprinkling of freckles on her face,
Surprisingly added to her grace.
We were freshmen together at W.V.U.,
Which is well remembered by more than a few.
Physical Ed was our course of study,
I realized now I had a buddy.
Preparing ourselves along the same line,
With a common interest making it fine.
It is so important for such a base,
To be enhanced by extra grace.
My Reggie gal has it all,
My life with her has been a ball.

Reggie and Ben. Courtesy of Reggie Schwartzwalder.

'59 Reunion at the Dome. Courtesy of Gerhard Schwedes.

22

Greatest Teams

When discussing the great teams in the history of college football, the 1959 Syracuse team typically ranks (depending on who's talking) in the lower part of the Top Ten, if at all. Many rate the 1971 Nebraska Cornhuskers as the best, others look at the Oklahoma dynasty in the mid 1950s, or the 1972 Southern California team as the measure of greatness. In some people's eyes, Red Blaik's Army teams of 1944–45 with Glenn Davis and Doc Blanchard provide the yardstick for perfection. Still others point to the great Miami teams of the last few years.

All of those teams were great, but when you look at Syracuse's total domination of college football in 1959, it's quite astonishing. The team finished the season 10–0, ranked first in both the AP and UPI polls, and was a unanimous choice for National Champion. The team led the nation in total offense and total defense, no team has ever did that before nor has any done it since. Statistically, Syracuse also led the nation in rushing offense, rushing defense, scoring, and touchdown passes. The Orange, in the entire season, gave up a measly 59 points, shutting out five teams while defeating its three toughest opponents away from home: UCLA before a nationally televised audience, 36–8; Penn State 20–18; and fourth-ranked Texas 23–14 in Dallas in the 1960 Cotton Bowl.

Some people point to a weak schedule, but when you compare schedules among the so called 'Greatest Teams,' you find that just isn't so. Syracuse's opponents were 59–49–2 for the '59 season, a winning percentage of 54.5. In comparison, the Oklahoma teams of 1955–56 went undefeated, a perfect 21–0. In 1955 their opponents were 46–62–2 for a winning percentage of 43.2. In 1956 it was worse. Their opponents were 32–63–6 for a winning percentage of 34.7. Coach Bud Wilkerson's teams shutout 11 opponents over that two-year span. The Sooners, led by halfback Tommy McDonald and center Jerry Tubbs, faced their toughest opponent in the 1956 Orange Bowl, third-ranked Maryland. After trailing 6–0 at halftime, Oklahoma came back to win 20–6 and claim another national championship.

Another team rated among the finest of all time is Southern Cal's 1972 squad led by All-Americans Lynn Swann and Charles Young. The Trojans were a perfect 13–0. Their opponents that year went 69–62–1, a winning percentage of 52.7. The Trojans were ranked in the Top Ten in the country in both offensive and defensive categories. Three of their players were selected in the first round of the NFL draft: Charles Young, fullback Sam Cunningham, and offensive lineman Pete Adams. Outstanding receiver Lynn Swann was selected in the second round and went onto a Hall of Fame career with the Pittsburgh Steelers.

Army's 1945 team had a perfect 9–0 record, led the nation in total offense, and ranked 10th in total defense. None of their opponents had losing records and had a combined record of 53–22–3, for a remarkable winning percentage of 69.9. (In 1944 the opponents winning percentage was also impressive 55.0) Army, led by Davis and Blanchard, beat previously undefeated Navy that year. Victories included Notre Dame (48–0), Michigan (28–7) and two military bases, Louisville AAF (32–0) and Melville R.I. (55–13). Louisville AAF and Melville RI have not been heard from since.

The 1971 Nebraska Cornhuskers, considered by many the greatest college football team, were a perfect 13–0 and unanimous choice for National Champion. Their opponents that year were a combined 83–63–1 for a winning percentage of 56.8. Their toughest opponent in 1971 was Oklahoma (11–1), a team they defeated on the road,

35–31, in what is arguably the best college football game of all time. Coach Bob Devaney's team ranked eighth in total offense, fifth in total defense, and third in both scoring offense and defense. Led by All-American halfback Johnny Rodgers (who would win the Heisman Trophy the following season), the Cornhuskers beat four top-twenty teams.

This book is not written in an effort to anoint the Orangemen of 1959 the greatest team ever. Because of personal biases and certain prejudices that can't be decided fairly. Football in the thirties was as different from football in the forties as football in the fifties was from that of the sixties, and so on right on down the line. The continued improvement in training methods, workout facilities, number of scholarships, equipment, and medical procedures, along with rule changes, bigger coaching staffs, and kids playing organized football at a younger age, all prepared athletes better as the years passed. But the Syracuse team in 1959 played the game as well as anybody ever. They dominated the college game as no other team ever has, and they've earned their rightful place in history.

College football will always be exciting and, thankfully, new teams will come forth that will be given "The Greatest Team Ever" title. They probably all will be worth the consideration. But we know in our hearts that somewhere out beyond the stars there's an old coach with a yellow pad doodling plays and a young black man running free and smiling who would beg to differ.

ANDERSON   EASTERLY

SCHWEDES   R. DAVIS

SYRACUSE

BEMILLER   HOWELL

GILBURG   GODFREY

GERHARD SCHWEDES, No. 16, Back

A veteran senior back who led the squad in rushing (360 yards) and pass-receiving (13) last year, Ger is a key figure on the current Orange team. Born in Germany, he now resides in Whitehouse, N. J.

JAMES ANDERSON, No. 35, Back

Jim is from nearby Oneonta, N. Y. A senior, he has performed two years as a reserve fullback. A tricky runner, Jim is a threat every time he carries the ball.

RICHARD EASTERLY, No. 49, Back

A Syracuse native who prepared at North High, Dick rates as a fine prospect at either halfback or quarterback, needing only game experience. Last spring he performed creditably with the baseball team in the late games.

ROGER DAVIS, No. 69, Guard

A leading All-America candidate, Rog is a senior with two seasons' fine play to his credit. Rated by most observers as Syracuse's best lineman, he' 6' 3", 228 pound and agile. He's from Solon, O.

ALBERT BEMILLER, No. 59, Center

A one-time end, Al moved to center last year as a sophomore and proved his merit. A much-improved performer this year, he should be one of the line standouts. A native of Hershey, Pa., 6', 4" and 202 pounds.

THOMAS GILBURG, No. 87, End

Rangy, talented junior from Chappaqua, N. Y., Tom saw much service last year. He is one of the nation's best collegiate punters, ranking second in the East in 1958 behind Syracuse's Ed Keiffer with a 39.4 average.

OTIS GODFREY, No. 67, Guard

Stocky, good-blocking forward from Weymouth, Mass., Godfrey is a junior who may see action this fall after getting experience with last year's Orange Bowl squad. He's due to be at left guard, behind Rog Davis.

JOHN HOWELL, No. 86, End

Last year, a sophomore reserve, John grabbed a touchdown pass in the Cornell game. He will add strength to the current flank corps. A native of Woodbridge, N. J., he played third base on the Syracuse baseball team.

Player bio's from 1959 game program. Courtesy of Syracuse University Archives.

YATES

SARETTE

HART

YOUMANS

SYRACUSE

APPLEHOF

SKONIECZKI

J. BROWN

SULLIVAN

ROBERT YATES, No. 79, Tackle

A Montpelier, Vt., product, husky Bob was one of the stalwarts on last year's Orange Bowl team. An inside tackle, he also is a fine, long-range, left-footed placekicker who booted the key field goal in last year's 16-13 victory over Pittsburgh.

DAVID SARETTE, No. 23, Back

As a quarterback candidate, Sarette's progress will be important to Orange success this season. He was the regular frosh quarter two years ago, but sat out the '58 campaign. Dave prepared at Central High in Manchester, N. H.

ROBERT HART, No. 19, Back

Elusive, speedy Bob is in his second season on the varsity squad. As a reserve righthalf last year he tallied one T.D. One of the squad's few married men. His home town is Bellevue, O.

MAURICE YOUMANS, No. 78, Tackle

Maury is a rangy, hard-working senior from nearby Mattydale who moved from end to an interior line post last season with fine results. This season he has been shifted to outside tackle, the post vacated by All-America Ron Luciano.

DAVID APPLEHOF, No. 53, Center

A native of Berea, O., Dave was last year's first-string center by virtue of his blocking and steadiness. On the small side for a lineman, this season he faces stern competition from Al Bemiller. Applehof also rates as an able tennis player.

GERALD SKONIECZKI, No. 88, End

Gerry is a stylish, senior end who snared five passes last year and scored one T.D. He was a standout performer against Oklahoma in the Orange Bowl. Played high school football at Johnson City.

JOHN BROWN, No. 76, Tackle

A resident of Camden, N. J., John is a speedy lineman with fine potential. He was out of varsity action last year, but his practice performances this season may earn him a high ranking among the tackles.

DANIEL SULLIVAN, No. 18, Back

Red-headed Dan is an up-and-coming sophomore right halfback who has good running ability. Last year he paired with Ernie Davis as the freshman halfbacks. Sullivan is from Dover, N. H.

Player bio's from 1959 game program. Courtesy of Syracuse University Archives.

A. BAKER

WEBER

TARBOX

REIMER

SYRACUSE

STEM

BARTLETT

F. MAUTINO

NICHOLS

ARTHUR BAKER, No. 39, Back

Husky, speedy Art logged a 4.7 average gaining 295 yards last year as a sophomore. Possibly Syracuse's most-improved back this year, Baker is an all-around athlete, performing in track and wrestling. He is the Eastern heavyweight and National 191-pound wrestling champion.

MARK WEBER, No. 46, Back

A reserve right half last year in his sophomore campaign, Mark has been shifted to left half this year and is expected to be a key ball-carrier. An engineering student from Solon, O., he scored Syracuse's touchdown in the Orange Bowl.

BRUCE TARBOX, No. 68, Guard

Bruce is due to be Rog Davis' running mate at the guard posts on the basis of his fine play last year as a sophomore. A one-time end, he played good football last year until injured. A graduate of the Kent School, Tarbox is the son of Bill Tarbox, former Syracuse lacrosse star.

RICHARD REIMER, No. 17, Back

Dick is on the, small side (168 pounds), but he's elusive and determined. Last year, as sophomore right half, he scored 26 points operating behind Ger Schwedes. One of the team's most dependable performers. A resident of Northampton, Pa.

ROBERT STEM, No. 56, Center

Bob was a star performer at center with last year's freshman team and is expected to give veterans Al Bemiller and Dave Applehof a battle at the pivot post. He's from Phillipsburg, N. J., the home of Jim Ringo, one-time Syracuse star now with the Green Bay Packers.

RONALD BARTLETT, No. 83, End

Ron is a rangy senior letterman at end who had gained valuable experience over the past two falls. He showed well in early workouts this year and may help fill the gap caused by the unexpected loss of Dave Baker, last year's regular flankman. Bartlett is from Amityville, N. Y.

FRED MAUTINO, No. 82, End

A returning regular, Fred grabbed six passes last year for two T.D.'s and is a crack defensive flankman. He played at Reading, Pa., High.

JOHN NICHOLS, No. 36, Back

A Cortland product, John has been moved to fullback after service last year at center when he developed into a capable line-backer. A junior, he has speed and agility.

Player bio's from 1959 game program. Courtesy of Syracuse University Archives.

BROKAW

GERLICK

E. DAVIS

FRANKOVITCH

SYRACUSE

ERICSON

GRABOWSKY

FEIDLER

GILL

ERNEST DAVIS, No. 44, Back

Ernie is a sophomore left halfback who has the potential to become an outstanding player. At 6', 2" and 205 pounds he has speed and hitting power. Gained more than 100 yards in three of four frosh games last year. Was an all-around scholastic star at Elmira Free Academy.

PETER BROKAW, No. 29, Back

A sophomore quarterback prospect from Nyack, Pete could become a top signal-caller with experience. A one-time halfback, he is fast and showed exceptional promise as last year's freshman quarterback.

ALBERT GERLICK, No. 77, Tackle

Stocky, 214-pound senior lineman who has gained nickname of "Cannonball" from his mates. A fine defensive player and able place-kicker. He's expected to alternate at inside tackle with Bob Yates.

GEORGE FRANCOVITCH, No. 62, Guard

One of last year's outstanding freshman linemen, Francovitch is rated a good prospect to earn the No. 2 spot at right guard behind Bruce Tarbox. He's from Ridgefield Park High and Little Ferry, N. J.

KENNETH ERICSON, No. 81, End

Ken is a rangy sophomore who transferred to Syracuse from West Point. He impressed during practice sessions with his speed and all-around ability. Formerly played at Weymouth, Mass., High.

RICHARD FEIDLER, No. 63, Guard

Dick, a sophomore, is a one-time end from Erie, Pa., who was moved to guard in spring practice where he showed considerable promise. He will vie with the veteran Otis Godfrey for the spot behind Rog Davis.

GLENN GILL, No. 73, Tackle

A reserve last year, Gill is an improved lineman who may see more duty this season. A 200-pounder, he is from Phillipsburg, N. J., High School.

EUGENE GRABOSKY, No. 72, Tackle

Syracuse's biggest player at 250 pounds, Gene showed considerable improvement late last season and could be a factor in this year's games. A senior, he lives in nearby Liverpool.

Player bio's from 1959 game program. Courtesy of Syracuse University Archives.

Dave APPELHOF

CENTER

One of the great things that '59 team personified is team spirit. I don't think I've ever been a part of a team that came together like that team did. We had fun but boy when you got in the locker room, you got ready to play, we played ball. We were not the greatest athletes in the world, but we became the greatest college football team in the world."

Gerhard SCHWEDES

HALFBACK

How do you measure the success of our team? I think because we cared about each other. It's amazing what you can accomplish when everyone pulls together. Every reunion thirty, forty guys from all over the country show up. Al Gerlick pulls it together. We have a bond. Well, I can't compare it. I can tell you what every one of the guys is doing in his life, I can tell you their wives' names. We are so damned close it is ridiculous.

"Ted Dailey said after the Cotton Bowl, 'You guys have no idea what you have just accomplished.' He said as long as you live and the longer you live, you are really going to appreciate being a National Championship Football team, and he was absolutely right. I wouldn't go anywhere without my National Championship Ring. First thing I put on in the morning is that ring. People ask me what's that ring, and I'm happier than hell to tell them. He was absolutely right."

1959 Syracuse University Football Team Statistics

The 1959 team was first in the Nation in the following categories:

Total offense	451.5 yards
Rushing	313.6 yards
Scoring	39.0 points
Total Defense	96.2 yards
Rushing Defense	19.3 yards
Touchdowns	21